Essential Histories

The Arab-Israeli Conflict
The Palestine War 1948

Essential Histories

The Arab-Israeli Conflict

The Palestine War 1948

OSPREY
PUBLISHING

Efraim Karsh

First published in Great Britain in 2002 by Osprey Publishing,
Elms Court, Chapel Way, Botley, Oxford OX2 9LP, UK
Email: info@ospreypublishing.com

ISBN 1 84176 372 1

Editor: Sally Rawlings
Design: Ken Vail Graphic Design, Cambridge, UK
Cartography by The Map Studio
Index by Alison Worthington
Picture research by Image Select International
Origination by Grasmere Digital Imaging, Leeds, UK
Printed and bound in China by L. Rex Printing Company Ltd.

02 03 04 05 06   10 9 8 7 6 5 4 3 2 1

For a complete list of titles available from Osprey Publishing
please contact:

Osprey Direct UK, PO Box 140,
Wellingborough, Northants, NN8 2FA, UK.
Email: info@ospreydirect.co.uk

Osprey Direct USA, c/o MBI Publishing,
PO Box 1, 729, Prospect Ave,
Osceola, WI 54020, USA.
Email: info@ospreydirectusa.com

www.ospreypublishing.com

Contents

Introduction

On 29 November 1947, the United Nations General Assembly passed a resolution calling for the partition of Palestine into two independent states – one Jewish, the other Arab – linked in an economic union. The City of Jerusalem was to be placed under an international régime, with its residents given the right to citizenship in either the Jewish or the Arab states. Thirty-three UN members supported the resolution, 13 voted against and 10 abstained, including Great Britain, which had ruled Palestine since the early 1920s under a League of Nations Mandate.

For Jews all over the world this was the fulfilment of a millenarian yearning for national rebirth in the ancestral homeland. For Arabs it was an unmitigated disaster, an act of betrayal by the international

The Middle East, 1948

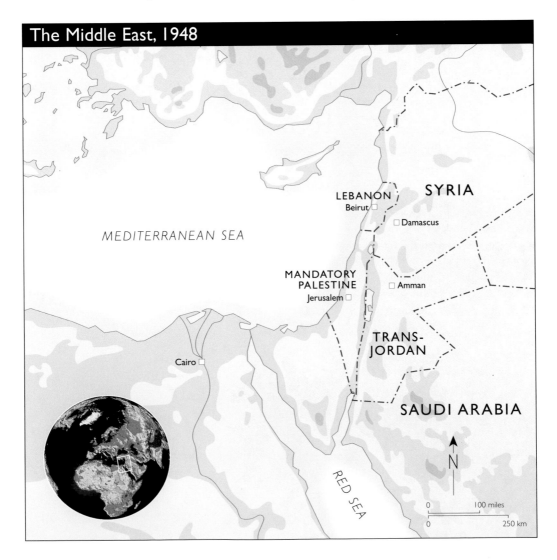

community that surrendered an integral part of the Arab world to foreign invaders. In Tel-Aviv, crowds were dancing in the streets. In the Arab capitals there were violent demonstrations. 'We are solidly and permanently determined to fight to the last man against the existence in our country of any Jewish state, no matter how small it is,' Jamal al-Husseini, Vice-President of the Arab Higher Committee (AHC), the effective government of the Palestinian Arabs, told the General Assembly as it was about to cast its vote. 'If such a state is to be established, it can only be established over our dead bodies.' And an AHC circular was even more outspoken. 'The Arabs have taken into their own hands the final solution of the Jewish problem,' it read. 'The problem will be solved only in blood and fire. The Jews will soon be driven out.'

Thus began the Palestine War, probably the most important Middle-Eastern armed confrontation since the destruction of the Ottoman Empire and the creation of a new regional order on its ruins in the wake of the First World War. It was to be divided into two distinct phases. The first began on 30 November 1947, the day after the adoption of the Partition Resolution, and ended on 14 May 1948 with the termination of the British Mandate. It was essentially a civil war, conducted under the watchful eye and occasional intervention of the British Mandatory authorities, in which the Palestinian Arab community, assisted by a sizeable pan-Arab irregular force, sought to prevent its Jewish counterpart from laying the foundation of statehood in line with the UN resolution. The second phase started on the night of 14–15 May 1948, a few hours after the proclamation of the State of Israel, and involved a concerted attack by the armed forces of Egypt, Syria, Iraq, Transjordan, Lebanon, as well as a Saudi contingent, on the nascent Jewish state. It ended on 20 July 1949 with the signing of the last of the armistice agreements between Israel and its Arab neighbours.

By the time the fighting was over, Israel, albeit at the exorbitant human cost of 1 per cent of its population, had survived the Arab attempt to destroy it at birth and had asserted its control over wider territories than those assigned to it by the UN Partition Resolution. The Palestinian Arab community was profoundly shattered, with about half of its population becoming refugees in other parts of Palestine and the neighbouring Arab states. The political implications of what would come to be known in Arab political discourse as *al-Nakba*, 'the catastrophe,' would reverberate throughout the Middle East for decades. Already before the end of hostilities the president of Syria was overthrown by a military coup, while the king of Egypt followed suit in the summer of 1952. Within two years of the end of the Palestine War, King Abdallah of Jordan, the foremost Arab combatant during the conflict, was assassinated, as were the prime ministers of Egypt and Lebanon. For decades inter-Arab politics would be dominated by the 'problem of Palestine' as the Arab states and the Palestinians sought to undo the consequences of the Palestine War and bring about Israel's demise by military, political and economic means. 'Palestine and the self-respect of the Arabs must be recovered,' the prominent Palestinian leader Musa Alami wrote in 1949. 'Without Palestine there is no life for them.'

Chronology

1917   **2 November** British Government issues the 'Balfour Declaration' supporting 'the establishment in Palestine of a national home for the Jewish people'

1920   **March** Britain awarded the Mandate for Palestine at the San Remo conference
April Arab riots in Jerusalem. Five Jews killed and 211 wounded

1921   **March** British Government excludes Transjordan from the prospective Jewish national home (though not from the Palestine Mandate)
April Hajj Amin al-Husseini appointed Mufti of Jerusalem
May Arab riots in Palestine. Ninety Jews killed and hundreds wounded

1922   **June** A British White Paper depreciates the nature of the prospective national Jewish home; limits Jewish immigration to the 'economic absorption capacity of the country'

1929   **August** Arab rioters kill 133 Jews and wound hundreds more

1930   **October** A White Paper recommends harsh restrictions on Jewish immigration and purchase of land

1936   **April** A 10-member Arab Higher Committee established as the effective leadership of the Palestinian Arabs; a general Arab uprising begins
October Uprising temporarily suspended at the request of Arab leaders

1937   **July** A Royal Commission of Inquiry, headed by Lord Peel, recommends the termination of the Mandate and the partition of Palestine into two states: an Arab state, united with Transjordan, in some 85 per cent of this territory, and a Jewish state in the rest. Jerusalem, Bethlehem, and a corridor leading them to the Mediterranean Sea to remain a British Mandatory zone

1938   **November** Woodhead Royal Commission: recommends the shelving of the Peel Partition Plan

1939   **May** A White Paper restricts Jewish immigration to no more than 15,000 per year during the next five-year period; after that it would occur only with Arab consent. Purchase of land by Jews is prohibited in some areas, restricted in others

1942   **May** A Zionist conference at the Biltmore Hotel, New York, demands that 'Palestine be established as a Jewish Commonwealth integrated in the structure of the new democratic world'

1946   **1 May** An Anglo-American Commission of Inquiry recommends the opening of Palestine to 100,000 Jewish refugees. Recommendation rejected by British Foreign Secretary Ernest Bevin
June A pan-Arab summit in Bludan (Syria) adopts a series of measures to prevent the creation of a Jewish state

1947   **March** Britain refers the Palestine problem to the UN
31 August UN Special Committee on Palestine (UNSCOP) recommends the earliest possible termination of the British Mandate. A majority report suggests the partition of Palestine into an Arab state, a Jewish state, and an internationalised city of Jerusalem – all linked in an economic union. A minority report recommends an independent federal state

16–19 September Pan-Arab summit in Sofar (Lebanon). Urges the Arab states to 'open their doors to Palestinian children, women, and the elderly and fend for them, should the developments in Palestine so require'

29 November UN General Assembly endorses UNSCOP's majority recommendation on the partition of Palestine

30 November Arab violence begins. Eight Jews killed, others wounded

1 December AHC proclaims a three-day nationwide strike

2 December Arab mob destroys the new Jewish commercial centre in Jerusalem

4 December Arabs attack on Efal: the first large-scale attempt to storm a Jewish neighbourhood. Failed

8 December Arab assault on Hatikva quarter in south Tel-Aviv. Failed with heavy casualties

8–17 December Arab League summit in Cairo. Decides to contribute one million Egyptian pounds and 10,000 rifles to the Palestine war effort

12 December Jewish car bomb near the Old City in Jerusalem. Twenty Arabs killed and five wounded

14 December Arab Legion attacks a Jewish supply convoy to Ben-Shemen, killing 12 people

18 December Eight Arabs killed in a Jewish retaliatory action against the Galilean village of Khasas

30 December Irgun bomb kills six Arab workers near the Haifa oil refinery. Arab workers at the plant kill 39 Jewish workers

1948 4 January Lehi blows up the headquarters of the Jaffa National Committee

10 January Arab Liberation Army (ALA) attack on Kfar-Szold. Failed

14 January Large-scale Arab attack on Etzion Bloc. Failed with heavy casualties

15–16 January A platoon of 35 Jewish fighters sent to reinforce Etzion Bloc wiped out

20 January ALA attack on Yechiam. Failed

1–15 February Jewish retaliatory strikes in Haifa, Jerusalem and Sasa

16 February ALA offensive against Tirat-Zvi. Failed with heavy casualties

22 February Arab car bomb explodes in Jewish Jerusalem. Fifty people killed, hundreds wounded

2–4 March Arab attacks on Magdiel and Ramot-Naftali. Failed

11 March Arab car bomb destroys Jewish national headquarters in Jerusalem

17 March Large Arab arms convoy destroyed in a battle near Haifa

19 March US proposes suspension of Partition Plan and a temporary international trusteeship for Palestine

27 March Jewish convoy from Nahariya to Yechiam ambushed. Forty-two fighters killed

27–28 March A large Jewish convoy returning from Etzion Bloc to Jerusalem ambushed near Nabi Daniel. Jewish fighters evacuated by British army. Weapons and vehicles lost to Arabs

31 March Jewish convoy to Jerusalem ambushed. Seventeen people killed

6–15 April Operation Nachshon: Jewish offensive to open the road to Jerusalem

4–12 April ALA offensive against Mishmar-Haemek. Failed with heavy losses

8 April The prominent Palestinian military commander Abd al-Qader al-Husseini killed

9 April Irgun and Lehi forces occupy Deir Yasin. Some 100 people killed

10 April Muslim Brothers attack Kfar-Darom. Failed

13 April Arabs ambush Jewish medical convoy in Jerusalem. Some 80 nurses and doctors killed

13–16 April Druze offensive against Ramat-Yohanan. Failed

15–21 April Operation Harel: three large supply convoys break through to Jewish Jerusalem

18 April Tiberias falls to the Hagana. Arab population evacuated at their request

21–22 April Haifa captured by the Hagana. Arab leaders refuse to surrender and order the evacuation of the city's Arab population

22–30 April Operation Jebusite: Jewish offensive to secure outlying Jerusalem neighbourhoods. Failed to occupy Nabi Samuel; seized Sheikh Jarrah but relinquished control at British demand; captured Qatamon

1–12 May Arab attacks on Galilee kibbutzim (Dan, Dafna, Kfar-Szold, Ramot-Naftali, Maayan-Baruch). Failed. Operation Yiftach: Hagana captures Arab villages and towns in eastern Galilee in anticipation of the Arab invasion

4–15 May Operation Barak: capture of Arab villages in the southern sector, in preparation for Arab invasion

8–18 May Operation Maccabee: Jewish offensive to clear the road to Jerusalem. Partial success

11 May Jewish forces capture Safed

11–12 May Muslim Brothers attack on Kfar-Darom. Failed

12 May Jewish forces occupy Beisan

13 May Jaffa surrenders to the Hagana. Arab Legion occupies the Etzion Bloc. Dozens of civilians and fighters killed after surrendering

14 May Termination of the British Mandate over Palestine. Proclamation of the State of Israel

15 May Armies of Egypt, Syria, Transjordan, Lebanon, and Iraq invade Israel. Egyptian air force bombs Tel-Aviv. Egyptian attacks on Kfar-Darom and Nirim. Failed

15–22 May Iraqi attacks on Gesher and the castle of Belvoir. Failed

17 May Egyptian forces enter Beersheba. Move northwards to the outskirts of Jerusalem

16–19 May Israeli raids on military targets in Syria and Lebanon

17–18 May Israeli forces capture Acre

18 May Syrian forces occupy Zemakh, Masada and Shaar-Hagolan

20 May Large-scale Syrian assault on Deganiya. Failed with heavy casualties. UN appoints Count Folke Bernadotte of Sweden as Mediator for Palestine

19–24 May Egyptian attack on Yad-Mordechai. Settlement captured after defenders' withdrawal

21–25 May Egyptian–Transjordanian attack on Ramat-Rahel. Failed

21–27 May Egyptian attack on Negba. Failed

22 May Israeli forces complete occupation of western Galilee

24 May Israeli forces recapture Shaar-Hagolan and Masada

25 May An Iraqi attack in the direction of Netanya. Failed. Operation Ben-Nun A: Israeli attack on the Latrun fortress. Failed with heavy casualties

28 May The Israel Defence Forces (IDF) established. Jewish Quarter in the Old City of Jerusalem falls to Arab Legion

30 May Operation Ben-Nun B: Second Israeli attack on Latrun. Failed

2 June Egyptian attack on Negba. Failed

3–4 June Israeli forces occupy Jenin. Dislodged by Iraqis

6 June Combined Syrian–Lebanese–ALA force captures Malkiya

6 June First convoy to Jerusalem through Burma Road

6–7 June Egyptian forces occupy Nitzanim, some 30 kilometres south of Tel-Aviv

7–8 June Operation Yitzhak: Israeli attack on Isdud. Failed

9 June Iraqi army occupies the head-waters of the Yarkon River at Ras el-Ein

10 June Syrians occupy Mishmar-Hayarden. Fail to capture Ein-Gev and Ramot-Naftali

9–10 June Operation Yoram: Third Israeli attack on Latrun. Failed

10–11 June Israeli forces capture a number of villages in southern sector but fail to occupy the strategic police fort of Iraq Sueidan

11 June Four-week truce begins

8 July Egyptians resume fighting. Kfar-Darom vacated

9–14 July Operation Brosh: Israeli attempt to dislodge Syrians from Mishmar-Hayarden. Failed

9–18 July Operation Dekel: IDF capture central Galilee (Nazareth falls on 16 July)

10 July Iraqis drive the IDF from the Jenin environs

10–15 July Egyptian attack on Negba, Beerot-Yitzhak, Julis, and Ibdis. Failed with heavy casualties

11–12 July Operation Danny: IDF captures Lydda, Ramle, and a string of Arab villages in the central front, including Ras el-Ein. Failed to occupy Latrun

16–17 July Operation Qedem: Israeli attempt to break into the Old City. Failed

17–18 July Operation 'Death to the Invader': IDF open a corridor to besieged Negev settlements

18 July Second truce begins

18 July–30 November Intermittent fighting in Jerusalem

22 July Egyptians block Israeli communications with the Negev

4–8 August Egyptians prevent Israeli convoys to the Negev in contravention of truce terms

17 September Bernadotte assassinated by the Lehi group. Ralph Bunche appointed Acting Mediator

20 September The 'Bernadotte Plan' published by the UN

15 October–5 November Operation Yoav: Israeli offensive drives Egyptians from the coastline and the Judean and Hebron Hills. Captures Beersheba and traps an Egyptian brigade in Faluja Pocket

29–31 October Operation Hiram: Israeli offensive expels ALA and Syrian forces from Upper Galilee. Sweeps into Lebanon

5 November The IDF captures Majdal and Yad-Mordechai

9 November IDF occupies Iraq Sueidan

22 December–2 January 1949 Operation Horev: IDF expel Egyptians from Israeli territory and invade the Sinai Peninsula. Withdrawal under international pressure

The burden of history

Wars are much like road accidents, the eminent British historian A. J. P. Taylor famously quipped. *They have a general cause and particular causes at the same time. Every road accident is caused, in the last resort, by the invention of the internal combustion engine and by men's desire to get from one place to another ... But a motorist, charged with dangerous driving, would be ill-advised if he pleaded the existence of motor cars as his sole defence. The police and courts do not weigh profound causes. They seek a specific cause for each accident – error on the part of the driver; excessive speed; drunkenness; faulty brakes; bad road surface. So it is with wars.*

Taylor was writing about the origins of the Second World War, but no modern-day conflict would seem to epitomise this intricate linkage between past and present more than the 1948 Palestine War. At a deeper level, the roots of this conflict stretch back to the Roman destruction of Jewish statehood in the land that has since come to be known as Palestine. Since then, exile and dispersion have become the hallmark of Jewish existence. Even in its ancestral homeland the Jewish community was relegated to a small minority under a long succession of foreign occupiers – Byzantines, Arabs, Seljuk Turks, Crusaders, Mamluks and Ottoman Turks – who inflicted repression and dislocation upon Jewish life. At the time of the Muslim occupation of Palestine in the seventh century, the Jewish community in the country numbered some 200,000; by the 1880s it had been reduced to about 24,000, or some five per cent of the total population.

This forced marginalisation notwithstanding, not only was the Jewish presence in Palestine never totally severed, but the Jews' longing for their ancestral

On 2 November 1917 the British Foreign Secretary, Arthur James Balfour, informed Lord Rothschild of his government's support for the 'establishment in Palestine of a national home for the Jewish people.' (Ann Ronan Picture Library)

homeland, or Zion, occupied a focal place in their collective memory for millennia and became an integral part of Jewish religious ritual. Moreover, Jews began returning to Palestine from the earliest days of dispersion, mostly on an individual basis, but also on a wide communal scale. The expulsion of the Jews from Spain in 1492, for example, brought in its wake a wave of new immigrants; an appreciable influx of religious Jews from eastern Europe occurred in the late eighteenth century, the same from Yemen 100 years later.

In the 1880s, however, an altogether different type of immigrant began arriving: the young nationalist who rejected diaspora life and sought to restore Jewish national existence in the historic homeland. Dozens of committees and societies for the settlement of the Land of Israel mushroomed in Russia and eastern Europe, to be transformed before long into a fully fledged political movement known as Zionism.

In August 1897 the First Zionist Congress was held in the Swiss town of Basle, under the chairmanship of Theodore Herzl, a young and dynamic Austro-Hungarian journalist. A milestone in modern Jewish and Middle-Eastern history, the congress defined the aim of Zionism as 'the creation of a home for the Jewish people in Palestine to be secured by public law'. It also established institutions for the promotion of this goal. By the outbreak of the First World War in 1914, the Jewish community in Palestine (or the Yishuv as it was commonly known) had grown to some 85,000–100,000 people, nearly 15 per cent of the total population.

Palestine at the time did not exist as a unified geopolitical entity; rather, it was divided between the Ottoman province of Beirut in the north and the district of Jerusalem in the south. Its local inhabitants, like the rest of the Arabic-speaking communities throughout the region viewed themselves as subjects of the Ottoman Empire rather than as members of a wider Arab Nation bound together by a shared language, religion, history or culture. They were totally impervious to the nationalist message of the handful of secret Arab societies operating throughout the empire prior to the First World War. Their immediate loyalties were parochial – to one's clan, tribe, village, town, or religious sect – which co-existed alongside their overarching submission to the Ottoman sultan-caliph in his capacity as the religious and temporal head of the world Muslim community.

Consequently, the growing Jewish presence in Palestine encountered no widespread opposition beyond the odd local dispute. Even the Balfour Declaration of

November 1917, in which the British Government endorsed 'the establishment in Palestine of a national home for the Jewish people' and pledged to 'use its best endeavours to facilitate the achievement of this object, it being clearly understood that nothing shall be done which may prejudice the civil and religious rights of existing non-Jewish communities in Palestine', generated no immediate antagonism. It took one full year for the first manifestation of local opposition to emerge in the form of a petition by a group of Palestinian dignitaries and nationalists proclaiming their loyalty to the Arab government established in Damascus in the wake of the First World War. But then, the head of the very government to which they swore their allegiance, Emir Faisal Ibn Hussein, the celebrated hero of the 'Great Arab Revolt' against the Ottoman Empire and the effective leader of the nascent Arab national movement, evinced no hostility towards the Balfour Declaration. On the contrary, in January 1919 he signed an agreement with Dr Chaim Weizmann, head of the Zionist movement, expressing support for 'the fullest guarantees for carrying into effect the British Government's Declaration of the 2nd November 1917' and for the adoption of 'all necessary measures ... to encourage and stimulate immigration of Jews into Palestine on a large scale'.

This is not what happened. No sooner had the ink dried on the agreement than Faisal, under the influence of his nationalist officers, reneged on this historic promise. Moreover, on 8 March 1920 the emir was crowned by his supporters as King Faisal I of Syria, 'within its natural boundaries, including Palestine', and the newly installed monarch had no intention of allowing the Jewish national movement to wrest away any part of

his kingdom. Indeed, the crowning ceremony was followed by violent demonstrations in Palestine as rumours spread regarding the country's imminent annexation to Syria. These culminated in early April 1920 in a pogrom in Jerusalem in which five Jews were killed and 211 wounded.

Though in July 1920 Faisal was overthrown by the French, his brief reign in Syria delineated the broad contours of the nascent Arab–Israeli conflict for decades to come. It did so by transforming the bilateral dispute between Arabs and Jews in Palestine into a multilateral Arab–Jewish conflict, and, no less importantly, by making physical force the foremost instrument of political discourse. In May 1921 Arab riots were renewed on a far wider scale than the previous year, leaving some 90 Jews dead and hundreds wounded. This paled in comparison to the wave of violence that erupted in the summer of 1929. Originating in religious incitement over Jewish prayers at the Wailing Wall, a remnant of King Solomon's Temple and Judaism's holiest site, Arab violence quickly spread from Jerusalem to engulf the entire country, resulting in the death of 133 Jews and the wounding of hundreds more. A particularly gruesome fate befell the ancient Jewish community of Hebron, dating back to biblical times, where 67 people were brutally slaughtered by their Arab neighbours, many dozens of others were wounded, property ransacked, and synagogues desecrated.

The driving force behind the violence was the young and militant religious leader Hajj Amin al-Husseini. Scion of a prominent Jerusalem family, Husseini served in the Ottoman army during the war, after which he became an ardent proponent of Palestine's incorporation into Greater Syria. Having played a major role in inciting the April 1920 riots, he was sentenced by a British military court to 15 years' imprisonment, but managed to flee the country, and in September 1920 was pardoned by Sir Herbert Samuel, the first British High Commissioner for Palestine. A year later, following the death of Kamil al-

Husseini, the Mufti of Jerusalem and his half-brother, Hajj Amin, presented his candidacy to the prestigious post. He failed owing to unsatisfactory religious credentials, but his family applied heavy pressure on the High Commissioner, with one of the three short-listed candidates stepping down in his favour. Having received Hajj Amin's pledge to use his family's prestige to restore calm to the country, Samuel relented and in April 1921 appointed him to Palestine's highest Islamic post. In January 1922 al-Husseini consolidated his power still further by establishing the Supreme Muslim Council (SMC), which oversaw all religious appointments in the country's Islamic community. In subsequent years, the Mufti quickly developed into the foremost Palestinian Arab political figure, cowering the feeble voices in favour of peaceful co-existence and putting his followers on a relentless collision course with the Zionist movement.

For quite some time this confrontational approach seemed to be working. Though accepting the Mandate for Palestine by March 1920, with a view to 'putting into effect the declaration originally made on November 2, 1917, by the British Government, and adopted by the other Allied Powers, in favour of the establishment in Palestine of a national home for the Jewish people,' the British quickly excluded the territory of Transjordan from the prospective Jewish national home (though not from the Palestine Mandate), making Emir Abdallah Ibn Hussein, Faisal's elder brother, the effective ruler of this territory. In June 1922 the British went further in distancing themselves from the Balfour Declaration by issuing a White Paper depreciating the nature of the prospective national Jewish home and seeking to limit Jewish immigration in line with the 'economic capacity of the country'. Eight years later, in response to the Arab riots of 1929, another White Paper advocated even harsher restrictions on immigration and land sales to Jews, though these recommendations were swiftly disowned by Prime Minister Ramsay MacDonald in response to Zionist pressure.

The Arabs remained defiant. In October 1933 a new cycle of violence erupted, followed three years later by a general uprising. By now the Mufti had consolidated his grip over Palestinian Arab politics and marginalised the more moderate elements within the leadership, headed by the Nashashibi clan. Capitalising on mounting Arab fears of Jewish immigration – which intensified in the early 1930s following the Nazi rise to power in Germany and rampant anti-Semitism in Poland – and on surging nationalist sentiments in the neighbouring Arab states, Hajj Amin had little difficulty in setting Palestine on fire. In April 1936 a 10-member Arab Higher Committee (AHC) was established as the effective national leadership, and an indefinite general strike was declared. This was accompanied by attacks on Jewish neighbourhoods throughout the country, as well as on British forces, by local guerrilla bands and Arab volunteers from the neighbouring countries, headed by Fawzi al-Qawuqji, a former officer in the Ottoman army.

In October 1936 the uprising was suspended at the request of a number of Arab leaders, notably Emir Abdallah of Transjordan, King Ghazi of Iraq and Saudi Arabia's King Abd al-Aziz Ibn Saud. In return, the British Government approved only 1,800 Jewish entry permits for the next six-month period, of the 11,200 requested by the Zionist movement. Far more importantly, a Royal Commission of Inquiry, headed by Lord Peel, was established to study the Palestine problem and to suggest possible ways for its resolution. When its recommendations were published in July 1937, they proved to be nothing short of revolutionary. Viewing Jewish and Arab national aspirations as irreconcilable under the terms of the Palestine Mandate, the commission suggested its abandonment and the partition of Palestine into two states: an Arab state, united with Transjordan, in some 85 per cent of this territory, and a Jewish state in the rest. Jerusalem, Bethlehem and a corridor leading them to the Mediterranean Sea were to remain a British Mandatory zone. To reduce future friction between the two communities, the commission proposed a land and population exchange between the Jewish and the Arab states, similar to that effected between Turkey and Greece in the wake of the First World War.

After a heated debate, the Zionist leadership gave the plan its qualified support. The AHC and the Arab governments dismissed it out of hand, insisting instead on the creation of an Arab-dominated unitary state in which the Jews would remain a small minority. The only Arab leader to have welcomed the plan was Abdallah, who viewed the unification between the prospective Arab state and Transjordan as a first step towards the vast Arab empire that he had been striving to create throughout his career.

The uprising was thus renewed with increased vehemence, only now it was also directed against the Mufti's internal Arab opposition, especially the Nashashibis. For their part, the British sought to calm the situation through the simultaneous use of the stick and the carrot. On the one hand, they suppressed the uprising with crude force – imposing collective punishments, bombarding villages and executing guerrillas. The AHC was outlawed, and the Mufti, who was sacked from the presidency of the Supreme Muslim Council, fled the country together with some of his leading chieftains.

At the same time, the British moved closer to the Arab position by backtracking on the idea of partition. Moreover, on 17 May 1939, as the clouds of war gathered over Europe, they issued yet another White Paper which restricted Jewish immigration to no more than 15,000 per year during the next five-year period; after that it would occur only with Arab consent. Purchase of land by Jews was prohibited in some areas, restricted in others. The White Paper also envisaged an independent state within a decade, in which the Jews would comprise no more than one-third of the total population.

World Jewry responded with vehement indignation to what it saw as the subversion of Jewish national revival in Palestine and the abandonment of European Jewry to their Nazi persecutor, as did a number of British politicians, such as the surviving members

of the Peel Commission and Winston Churchill, who viewed the White Paper as 'a low-grade gasp of a defeatist hour'. Yet the Arabs were not satisfied with this major achievement, demanding the immediate creation of an Arab state in Palestine, the complete cessation of Jewish immigration and a review of the status of every Jew who had entered the country after 1918.

The outbreak of the Second World War temporarily shelved this issue, but the

In the spring of 1936 the Palestinian Arabs mounted a general uprising, which was to continue intermittently for the next three years before being suppressed by the British authorities. Here British troops impose a curfew in the Old City of Jerusalem. (The State of Israel: The National Photo Collection)

struggle over the White Paper was resumed immediately after the war. Much to Jewish disappointment, not only did the Labour Government, which came to power in July 1945, fail to live up to its pre-election pro-Zionist stance but it turned out to be a bitter enemy of the Jewish national cause. The White Paper restrictions were thus kept in place and the Jews were advised by Foreign Secretary Ernest Bevin not 'to get too much at the head of the queue'. Dozens of

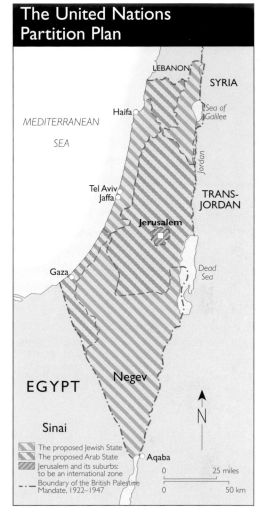

The United Nations Partition Plan

The proposed Jewish State
The proposed Arab State
Jerusalem and its suburbs: to be an international zone
Boundary of the British Palestine Mandate, 1922–1947

0   25 miles
0   50 km

thousands of Holocaust survivors who chose to ignore the warning and to brave the British naval blockade were incarcerated in Cyprus for years. When in August 1945 US President Harry Truman endorsed the Zionist demand for the immediate admission of 150,000 Jewish refugees into Palestine, Bevin sought to nip the idea in the bud by suggesting an Anglo-American Commission of Inquiry to 'examine what could be done immediately to ameliorate the position of the Jews now in Europe'. Yet when the following year the commission unanimously recommended the issue of 100,000 immigration certificates and the abolition of restrictions on Jewish purchase of land the British Government refused to comply.

The alarmed Zionists were quick to respond. Already on 6 May 1942, as news of the real magnitude of the Nazi atrocities began to filter through to Britain and the United States, and as the British Government was adamant that 'all practicable steps should be taken to discourage illegal immigration into Palestine', a Zionist conference at the Biltmore Hotel in New York decided that Britain could no longer be trusted to discharge its Mandatory obligations, and that 'Palestine be established as a Jewish Commonwealth integrated in the structure of the new democratic world.' Now that the Labour Government seemed to have vindicated this stark prognosis, the Zionist movement embarked on a combined military and political struggle for Jewish statehood. The foremost Jewish underground resistance organisation, the Hagana (Defence), resorted to shows of force such as the destruction of roads and bridges and obstruction of British anti-immigration measures, while the two small dissident organisations – Irgun Zvai Leumi (National Military Organisation) and Lehi (Fighters for Israel's Independence, better known as the 'Stern gang' after its commander, Avraham Stern) – waged an all-out assault on Britain's military and administrative institutions. At the political level the Zionists mounted an international political and diplomatic campaign for the partition of Palestine into two states – one Jewish, one Arab.

This was totally unacceptable to the Arabs. In May 1946, a pan-Arab summit in Cairo vowed to keep Palestine an integral part of the Arab world and denounced Zionism as 'a danger not only to Palestine but to all Arab and Muslim peoples'. The following month yet another general Arab summit in the Syrian town of Bludan adopted a series of measures to prevent the creation of a Jewish state, including anti-British and anti-American sanctions if the two powers implemented the recommendation of the Anglo-American commission and introduced 100,000 Jewish refugees into Palestine. Hajj Amin

al-Husseini, who returned to the Palestinian helm after having spent most of the war in Nazi Germany collaborating with Hitler, vowed from his Cairo headquarters that 'we would rather die than accept minority rights' in a prospective Jewish state. In a message to President Truman, King Ibn Saud warned that 'the Arabs are determined to wage war with the same determination and force as during the crusades', while the secretary-general of the Arab League, Abd al-Rahman Azzam, promised to 'defend Palestine no matter how strong the opposition and no matter what means are used by the partition supporters'. 'We will ultimately be victorious,' he vowed confidently. 'You will achieve nothing with talk of compromise or peace,' he told a secret delegation of peace-seeking Zionists in September 1947:

For us there is only one test, the test of strength ... We will try to rout you. I am not sure we will succeed, but we will try. We succeeded in expelling the Crusaders, but lost Spain and Persia, and may lose Palestine. But it is too late for a peaceable solution.

Azzam was completely wrong. The Zionist 'talk of compromise or peace' was making real international headway. On 15 May 1947, two months after the British Government had referred the Palestine problem to the newly established United Nations, the 11-member UN Special Committee on Palestine (UNSCOP) was established to study the question and to suggest possible ways for its resolution. In its recommendations, published at the end of August, the committee advocated the earliest possible termination of the British Mandate. The majority report recommended the partition of Palestine into an Arab state, a Jewish state, and an internationalised city of Jerusalem – all linked in an economic union. The minority report suggested an independent federal state, established after a transitional period of up to three years and comprising an Arab state and a Jewish state with Jerusalem as the federal capital. The Jews wholeheartedly endorsed the majority

recommendations. The Arab states and the AHC, re-established in 1946 under Hajj Amin's headship as the effective government of the Palestinian Arabs, rejected both proposals. Yet they were fighting a rearguard action. On 29 November 1947, the UN General Assembly endorsed UNSCOP's majority recommendation on the partition of Palestine by a two-thirds majority.

As Britain maintained a tight naval blockade around Palestine after the Second World War so as to prevent Jewish immigration, the Hagana sought to covertly smuggle many Holocaust survivors into the country. (The State of Israel: The National Photo Collection)

Strengths and weaknesses of Arabs and Jews

The 1948 Palestine War was no 'ordinary' confrontation between two combatants. Rather it was a complex multilateral conflict in which the Jewish community in Mandatory Palestine (or the Yishuv), then the newly proclaimed State of Israel, fought against three distinct, if interconnected, enemy forces: the Palestinian Arabs, a pan-Arab volunteer force and the regular armed forces of six Arab states – Egypt, Transjordan, Iraq, Syria, Lebanon, and a Saudi contingent.

To complicate things still further, in its capacity as the governing power in Palestine until the termination of the Mandate in mid-May 1948, Britain kept substantial military forces there and maintained official responsibility for the country's internal and external security. And while these forces neither played an active part in the Arab–Jewish military confrontation nor

seriously attempted to enforce nationwide law and order, their presence in the country had a major impact on the general course of the conflict. For one thing, it deterred the Arab states from sending their armies into Palestine prior to the termination of the Mandate. For another, the pattern and pace of the British withdrawal influenced Jewish and Palestinian operational planning and execution and at times even determined the outcome of critical military encounters, notably the battle for the strategic port town of Haifa. Not least, the tight British naval blockade around Palestine substantially weakened the Yishuv's war effort by preventing the influx of Jewish refugees and newly acquired weapons into the country.

The Jewish position

As it braced itself for the promised Arab backlash to the Partition Resolution, the Yishuv could hardly ignore its stark inferiority to the Arab World on every quantitative index of power, from demography, to territory, to geostrategic location, to wealth. Its 650,000-strong population was about half the size of the Palestinian Arab community, and less than three per cent of the population of those Arab states that had vowed to abort Jewish statehood by force. Its tenuous geographical disposition, with many villages dispersed in predominantly Arab areas, and the Arabs controlling most of Palestine's hill region and its major road arteries, made it vulnerable both to attacks on isolated neighbourhoods and to the disruption of communication between entire parts of the country. Moreover, Palestine's encirclement by four Arab states – Lebanon and Syria in the north, Transjordan in the east and Egypt in the south-west – made its Jewish community virtually landlocked and dependent for its very existence on naval and aerial transportation. But then, the port of Haifa, Palestine's primary naval outlet, was controlled by the British until their departure, while the country's sole civilian airport was a short distance from the Arab town of Lydda.

All this created a fundamental asymmetry between the positions of the Yishuv and its Arab adversaries. While the former could not afford a single strategic defeat, as it would inexorably lead to its destruction, the Arabs world could absorb successive setbacks and still remain, in Abd al-Rahman Azzam's words, 'fully confident of ultimate success though it might take some years. It would be a war of attrition since manpower reserves upon which the Arab side could draw were inexhaustible.' This prognosis

In an attempt to incorporate its diverse underground units into a unified force, on 28 May the Israeli Government ordered the establishment of a national army - the Israel Defence Forces (IDF). (Topham picturepoint)

was shared by the US intelligence agencies. 'The Jewish forces will initially have the advantage,' opined a report issued a day before the passing of the Partition Resolution. 'However, as the Arabs gradually co-ordinate their war effort, the Jews will be forced to withdraw from isolated positions, and having been drawn into a war of attrition, will gradually be defeated. Unless they are able to obtain significant outside aid in terms of manpower and matériel, the Jews will be able to hold out no longer than two years.'

What these predictions failed to consider, however, was the extraordinary resilience of

Established in the early 1920s as the underground military arm of the Palestine Jewish community, the Hagana (Defence) developed in subsequent decades into a well-organised and highly motivated movement. Here Hagana members training in Tel-Aviv. (The State of Israel: The National Photo Collection)

the Yishuv. A vibrant national community with an unwavering sense of purpose, it could rely on an extensive network of indigenous social, economic, financial, educational and military institutions that had turned it into a state in waiting. Chief of these were the Jewish Agency, created under the terms of the League of Nations Mandate for Palestine and led by an Executive which, over time, became the effective government of the Yishuv and of the worldwide Zionist movement; the elected Va'ad Leumi (or Representative Council) of Palestine's Jewish population; the Histadrut workers' organisation, and the semi-clandestine military arm of the Yishuv, the Hagana.

Established in the early 1920s in response to mounting Arab violence, the Hagana developed in subsequent decades into a well-organised and highly motivated underground movement. Subordinated to the Yishuv's civilian leadership, on the eve of the 1948 War its political control was in the hands of David Ben-Gurion, Chairman of the Jewish Agency and soon to become the first prime minister of the new State of Israel. Professional military control was exercised by an underground general staff of some 400 full-time salaried activists who constantly evaded the watchful eyes of the British.

The Hagana's foremost unit was the Palmach (Plugot Mahatz, or shock platoons), an elite force established in 1941 when the spectre of a German invasion of Palestine loomed large. In late 1947, it included some 2,100 men and women on active duty, plus 1,000 trained reservists who had returned to civilian life but could be recalled at a moment's notice. It was supported by a 12,000-strong infantry force (2,000 on active service and 10,000 reserves) called the Hish (Heil Sadeh, or field force). Comprising men of 18–25 voluntarily devoting weekends and vacations to military training, the Hish's largest tactical unit was the company, and the normal unit of training or operation was the platoon.

On top of its field units, the Hagana had a 20,000-strong garrison force, the Him (Heil Mishmar, or guard force), consisting of men and women of 25 and over who were unfit for combat units and were assigned to static defence missions, especially in villages throughout the country.

In terms of weaponry, the Hagana held at its secret caches (under Mandatory laws possession of arms was a crime punishable by death) some 10,000 rifles and 1,900 submachine guns: one weapon for every three fighters (even the Palmach could only arm two out of every three of its active members), as well as 186 medium machine guns, 444 light machine guns, and some 750 mortars. It had no heavy machine guns, artillery, armoured vehicles, or anti-tank and anti-aircraft weapons. Its nucleus air arm consisted of 11 single-engined light civilian aircraft, while its naval platoon included some 350 sailors with a few motor boats.

The other two underground Jewish organisations operating in Palestine at the time were far smaller in size and equipment. The Irgun numbered some 2,000–4,000 members, armed with 200 rifles, 500 submachine guns, and 160 machine guns, while the far smaller Lehi (500–800 members) had at its disposal some 130 submachine guns, 120 revolvers and no rifles at all.

Finally, there were a few thousand men and women who had served in the British army during the Second World War. They did not belong to any of the underground organisations, but their military experience would be of great help to the Yishuv during the war.

The Palestinian Arabs

In terms of social cohesion and organisation, the Palestinian Arab community was distinctly inferior to its smaller Jewish counterpart. Unlike the Yishuv it had totally failed to develop a corporate national identity, remaining instead an uncertain amalgam of internal schisms and animosities: between town dwellers and countrymen, Muslims and Christians, rival families, clans, tribes and so on. Moreover, the suppression of the 1936–39 uprising left Palestinian society economically weakened and politically leaderless with the collapse of its foremost institutions and the flight of its leadership to the neighbouring Arab countries. And while the AHC was reconstituted as the effective government of the Palestinian Arab community, Hajj Amin's loyal service on behalf of the Nazis during the war had largely discredited him in the eyes of the great powers.

No less importantly, despite their fiery rhetoric, the Arab régimes were far less concerned with defending the Palestinian Arabs than with promoting their own self-serving interests. Transjordan's King Abdallah was keen to incorporate the whole of Palestine into the Greater Syrian empire that he had been toiling to establish throughout his political career, while Egypt was anxious to prevent this eventuality and to wrest whatever parts of southern Palestine it could. Syria and Lebanon set their sights on certain areas in northern Palestine, while Iraq harboured its own ambition for the unification of the Fertile Crescent under its leadership.

Consequently, the Arab states were unwilling to allow the Mufti to lead the struggle for Palestine. He was excluded from the Arab League's deliberations in the run-up to the UN vote on partition, and in its wake he was denied command over the Palestine military campaign, which was entrusted to the Iraqi General Ismail Safwat under the supervision of the Arab League's newly established military committee. Yet another Iraqi general, Taha al-Hashemi, former chief of staff of the Iraqi army, was appointed commander of the Arab Liberation Army (ALA), a pan-Arab volunteer force established by the League in early 1948. His deputy and the person who would lead this force into battle was the Syrian Fawzi al-Qawuqji, veteran of the 1936–39 uprising. This constituted a double blow to the Mufti. Not only was this relatively efficient and well-equipped force placed under one of his erstwhile rivals (al-Qawuqji), but its very

creation deprived the Palestinians of much needed arms and funds that would have otherwise been transferred directly to them. All that the Mufti managed to achieve with great difficulty was the appointment of his two foremost protégés to key military positions: his nephew, Abd al-Qader al-Husseini, was made commander of the Jerusalem front, while Hasan Salame, a veteran of the 1936–39 uprising who had spent much of the war years in the service of the Nazis, was given command over the Lydda–Ramle area.

Nor did the Mufti manage to integrate Palestinian society into a comprehensive war fighting machine. While national committees were established in most towns and rural areas to control the war operations in their respective vicinities, the social and political fragmentation of Palestinian society turned the traditional local armed band into the regular fighting formation. Yet this by no means reduced to insignificance the potential military capabilities of Palestinian society. On the contrary, numerous Arab villagers carried weapons and could be called to action by the local sheikh or strong man at a moment's notice, and many of them had gained valuable experience in guerrilla warfare during the 1936–39 uprising. To this should be added the 7,500 Palestinians who had undergone combat training by the British during the Second World War, and the 10,500 Arabs serving in the British police force on either a full-time or auxiliary basis. As the situation deteriorated, many of these deserted their units with their weapons to join the numerous armed groups operating in the country.

On a more organised basis, the Palestinians had two paramilitary groups, the Husseini-sponsored Futuwa, and the Najada, which had been created by opponents of the Husseinis though eventually came under their sway and merged with the Futuwa. Both engaged in elementary training in urban guerrilla warfare and on the eve of their merger in July 1947 their joint strength totalled some 11,000–12,000 members, about a tenth of whom were ex-servicemen.

As hostilities broke out in late 1947, new local militia groups, commonly known as the National Guard, mushroomed in Palestinian towns and cities. Consisting of war veterans and members of existing organisations, they assumed responsibility for the defence of their specific neighbourhoods, taxing the local population for their upkeep and weaponry. Yet another militia, al-Jihad al-Muqadas (The Holy War), expanded rapidly from a modest group of a few hundred Palestinian war veterans and Arab volunteers, created by Abd al-Qader al-Husseini in early 1948, to a force boasting several thousand young Palestinians. They were supported by Hasan Salame's 1,000-strong force operating on the central front.

The lack of a centralised Palestinian organisation makes it difficult to assess their level of armament. Like the Yishuv, they had no major weapons systems such as fighting aircraft, tanks or artillery and were in possession of substantial quantities of small arms. As early as 1942, the Hagana's intelligence service assessed the number of firearms at the disposal of the Palestinians at 50,000; and while this was probably an overestimate, it nevertheless reflected the prevalence of private weapons in Palestinian society. In the wake of the Second World War, and especially as the spectre of partition loomed larger, the Palestinians intensified their arms procurement efforts. Most of their newly obtained weapons were smuggled from the neighbouring Arab states, while the rest were stolen from British military and police bases.

The Arab states

The material and organisational Palestinian weakness was more than compensated for by the combined strength of the Arab world. Unlike Palestine's Jewish and Arab communities which, by virtue of their imperial domination, could not develop regular armies or obtain major weapons systems, the Arab states, as independent entities, could and did precisely this. As a result, at the time of the 1948 War they were able to field well-organised and equipped armies, armed with tanks, artillery and fighting aircraft.

As the largest and most populous Arab country, Egypt had the most extensive military establishment. Supplied and trained by Britain, the Egyptian armed forces trebled their order of battle in the wake of the Second World War to 35,000–45,000 troops. The ground forces consisted of three infantry brigades, one tank brigade (with some 50 tanks) and three artillery battalions armed with 65 Howitzer guns, while the air force comprised five squadrons of 18 fighting aircraft each and one transport squadron.

Owing to the hegemonic aspirations of its rulers, Iraq had made a comparatively greater effort than any other Arab state in the development of its military potential. By 1948 its armed forces had expanded to approximately the same size as those of larger Egypt, but were better equipped, organised and trained. The main bulk of its ground forces was structured in three divisional formations – two infantry and one 'training' – supported by an armoured battalion of 15–20 tanks, some 200 armoured vehicles and 70–80 artillery pieces. The Iraqi air force consisted of 80 aircraft, about half of which were operational.

By far the most effective Arab force was Transjordan's Arab Legion. Armed, trained and commanded by British officers, this 10,000-strong force was organised in four infantry/mechanised regiments supported by some 40 artillery pieces and 75 armoured cars. Until January 1948, it was reinforced by the 3,000-strong Transjordan Frontier Force, at which time it was disbanded and its members joined the Arab Legion or other armed forces, many of them taking their arms with them.

The Syrian and Lebanese armies, both established by the French during their rule of the Levant, were apparently the weakest of the Arab interventionary forces. Totalling a mere 3,500 troops, the Lebanese army

consisted of four infantry brigades, a mechanised company, some cavalry units and a number of artillery pieces. The Syrian armed forces, though three times as large, were in the spring of 1948 in the midst of transition from an old-fashioned gendarmerie and cavalry force to a modern infantry division. As a result, only two of the division's three brigades were in a position to take part in the war, together with a mechanised battalion of French-built tanks and a modest air force of some 20 training aircraft converted into bombers and fighters.

Syria's contribution to the general war effort, however, extended well beyond its direct involvement as it played the key role in the creation of the ALA. Though hypothetically a pan-Arab force aimed at assisting the Palestinian struggle until the Arab states were able to send their armies into Palestine, it was Syria that provided the ALA with most of its officers, recruits, weapons and training. Envisaged as a divisional force, the ALA comprised, at its peak, some 8,000 fighters organised in six battalions and armed with light weapons, mortars and guns.

Armed, trained and commanded by British officers, Transjordan's 10,000-strong Arab Legion was by far the most effective Arab army to participate in the Palestine War. Here King Abdallah is inspecting a guard of Arab Legion soldiers. (The State of Israel: The National Photo Collection)

The British forces

At the time of the UN vote on partition, there were some 100,000 British troops deployed in Palestine, organised in two ground forces divisions, two independent infantry brigades, two mechanised regiments, some artillery units and a number of RAF squadrons. The élite 6th Airborne Division was deployed in northern Palestine, the 1st Infantry Division was in charge of the central and southern areas, including Tel-Aviv, Samaria, the coastal plain and the Negev (together with the 61st Infantry Brigade), while the Jerusalem area was the responsibility of the 8th Infantry Brigade. In addition, the Palestine Command had at its disposal the Arab Legion, the Transjordan Frontier Force, the naval units of the Mediterranean Fleet, and over 4,000 British members of the Palestine Police Force.

'The Arabs of Palestine will never submit to partition'

Violence came to Palestine within hours of the UN vote on partition. In the early hours of 30 November 1947 as Jewish revellers were making their way home after the previous night's celebrations, an ambulance en route to the Hadassah Hospital on Mount Scopus came under fire. A few hours later a group of Arabs ambushed a Jewish bus bound from the coastal town of Netanya to Jerusalem, killing five of its passengers and wounding several others. They then attacked another bus travelling from Hadera to Jerusalem, killing two more passengers.

Meanwhile, in Tel-Aviv's Carmel Market, on the fault line between the Jewish city and what was Arab Jaffa, a Jewish person was murdered. In the country's main gaol, in the northern town of Acre, Arab prisoners attacked Jewish inmates, who barricaded themselves in their cells until the British authorities managed to restore calm. In Haifa, shots were fired at Jews passing through Arab neighbourhoods, while Jewish vehicles were stoned throughout the country.

The next day saw no reduction in violence. Shooting, stoning and rioting continued apace. The consulates of Poland and Sweden, both of which had voted for partition, were attacked. Bombs were

Having spent most of the Second World War years in the service of Nazi Germany, the former Jerusalem Mufti, Hajj Amin al-Husseini (second from the left) arrived in Cairo in 1945 to lead the Palestinian Arab campaign against the partition of Palestine. (Topham Picturepoint)

thrown into cafés, killing and maiming, molotov cocktails were hurled at shops, a synagogue was set on fire. Scores of young Arabs flooded the offices of the local national committees demanding weapons. To inflame the situation further, the AHC proclaimed a three-day nationwide strike to begin the following day. It enforced the closure of all Arab shops, schools and places of business and organised and incited large Arab crowds to take to the streets to attack Jewish targets.

The main such attack took place in Jerusalem on Tuesday 2 December, when a crowd of several hundred Arabs ransacked the new Jewish commercial centre, lying opposite the Old City's walls, looting and burning shops and stabbing and stoning whoever they happened upon. A Hagana platoon that was rushed to the area to protect civilians was peremptorily stopped and disarmed by the British police, with 16 of its members arrested for illegal possession of weapons. Some of the confiscated weapons were later found on killed and captured Arab rioters.

From the commercial centre, the mob proceeded to the City Hall, where they attempted to lynch several Jewish municipal workers and to plunder nearby stores. 'For a long time the police did not interfere with this little mob,' recollected the city's British mayor, Richard Graves, 'and it was heartbreaking to see these young hooligans being given a free hand to destroy the products of man's labours ... I remonstrated with the police [who] told me that they had orders not to interfere till they were reinforced.'

On 4 December, some 120–150 armed Arabs attacked kibbutz Efal, on the outskirts of Tel-Aviv, in the first large-scale attempt to storm a Jewish settlement. Four days later a more audacious assault was launched when hundreds of armed Arabs attacked the Hatikva quarter in south Tel-Aviv. They were followed by scores of women, bags and sacks in hand, eager to ferry off the anticipated spoils. 'The scene was appalling,' recalled one of the Jewish defenders. 'Masses of Arabs

were running towards the neighbourhood. Some of them carried torches while others fired on the fly. Behind them we saw flashes of fire from machine guns covering them as they ran amok.' By the time the British troops arrived at the scene, the Arabs had been forced into a hasty retreat, leaving behind some 70 dead.

This failure notwithstanding, the Hatikva attack constituted a watershed in the general deterioration to war. Planned and executed by Hasan Salame, the Mufti-appointed commander of the Lydda front, and including an unspecified number of fighters who had arrived from Nablus to this end, the operation inaugurated a trend that was to gain momentum in the coming weeks, transforming the conflict from mob rioting and local clashes to a more orderly guerrilla campaign aimed at achieving specific objectives. Indeed, two days after the abortive Hatikva assault, yet another concerted Arab attack was rebuffed – this time on the Jewish Quarter of Jerusalem's Old City.

The Arab states

Violence was by no means confined to Palestine. Throughout the Arab world, Jewish communities were singled out for attack. In British-ruled Aden, 82 Jews were slaughtered by rioting mobs, while another 130 Jews were massacred in Tripolitania. In Beirut, Cairo, Alexandria and Aleppo Jewish houses and businesses were ransacked and synagogues desecrated.

Between 8 and 17 December the heads of the Arab states met in Cairo for a series of meetings, under the auspices of the Arab League, to discuss the Palestine situation. The gathering defined the overarching Arab objective as 'obstructing the partition plan, preventing the creation of a Jewish state, and preserving Palestine as an independent unified Arab state'. To this end, the Arab states would contribute one million Egyptian pounds to the Palestine war effort (on top of the same amount promised three months earlier by another Arab League summit in the Lebanese town of Sofar), would place some 10,000 rifles at the disposal of the League's military committee and would make the necessary arrangements for the recruitment of 3,000 volunteers for the ALA that was being established in Syria. They also reaffirmed the decision, taken at the Alei summit of October 1947, to deploy their forces along the Palestine border so long as the British remained in the country, in order to extend active support for the ALA's operations within Palestine.

The Jewish response

The outbreak of Arab violence did not take the Yishuv by surprise. Since assuming the defence portfolio in December 1946, in addition to the chairmanship of the Jewish Agency, David Ben-Gurion had been labouring under the assumption that upon the termination of the Mandate the Yishuv would have to confront the full military might of the Arab world, rather than that of the Palestinian Arabs alone. Consequently, in late 1947 and early 1948 the Hagana underwent a major structural change, aimed at transforming its semi-mobilised units into a national army based on compulsory conscription that would be able to resist an invasion by the regular Arab armed forces. Most notably, the Hish was restructured into five regional brigades: Levanoni in the northern part of the country (it later developed into two separate brigades – Carmeli and Golani); Alexandroni, with responsibility for the central sector; Givati in southern Palestine; and the Etzioni brigade in the Jerusalem area.

Nor did the actual pattern of the Palestinian violence come as a surprise. A month before the passing of the UN Resolution, Israel Galili, the Hagana's Chief of staff estimated that:

As far as we know, it is the Mufti's belief that there is no better way to 'start things off' than by means of terror, isolated bombs thrown into crowds leaving movie theatres on Saturday nights. That will start the ball rolling. For no doubt the Jews will react, and as a reaction to a reaction there will be outbreak in another place ... [until] the whole country will be stirred up, trouble will be incited, and the neighbouring Arab countries will be compelled to start a 'holy war' to assist the Palestinian Arabs.

To prevent this scenario from becoming a self-fulfilling prophecy, the Hagana's initial response to the outbreak of violence was essentially defensive, trying to strike a delicate balance between the need to create a credible deterrence and the desire to prevent the cycle of violence from spiralling to uncontrollable peaks. It was only on 9 December, as Arab attacks on Jewish transportation across the country began to have a palpable effect, that the Hagana's head of operations, Yigael Yadin, ordered commanders to respond in kind so as to curtail the Arab campaign against Jewish transportation.

In addition, the Hagana began to carry out retaliatory actions against specific targets, such as known perpetrators of violence, bases of armed gangs, and villages or localities serving as springboards for anti-Jewish attacks. One such action took place in Ramle on 11 December, when a Palmach squad managed to infiltrate the town and to set fire to 15 Arab vehicles in a parking lot. On another instance, an infantry platoon entered the southern village of Karatiya, which had been used as a base for attacks on Jewish traffic in the area, and blew up a building after evacuating its residents. A similar operation, in the Galilee village of Khasas went terribly wrong, as sappers miscalculated the amount of explosives needed for demolishing a building, causing the collapse of a neighbouring house and killing eight people.

While the Hagana did its utmost to avoid attacks on innocent civilians, the smaller Jewish underground organisations had no such scruples: if Jews were to be indiscriminately attacked throughout the country, so too would Arabs. Thus, hours after the Arab attack on the Jerusalem commercial centre on 2 December, the Irgun set fire to a Jerusalem cinema house frequented by Arabs. Ten days later, on 12 December, it placed a car bomb opposite the Damascus Gate of the Old City, killing

20 people and wounding another five. Lehi used the same method to blow up the headquarters of the Jaffa national committee on 5 January 1948.

On 30 December, a group of Irgun members threw a bomb at a group of Arab workers waiting outside the Haifa oil refinery, killing six people and wounding

others. Within hours the Arab workers at the plant turned on their Jewish colleagues, slaughtering 39 of them and injuring many more. In response, the Hagana raided the village of Balad al-Sheikh, from where many of the rioters came, killing and wounding some 60 people.

By the end of 1947, then, Palestine was in flames as Arabs and Jews were fighting each other in its towns, villages and on its roads. From the passing of the Partition Resolution on 29 November 1947 to the beginning of the new year, some 207 Jews and 220 Arabs were killed, according to official British figures, while several hundred others were wounded.

Violence came to Palestine on 30 November 1947, a day after the UN had passed the Partition Resolution. Here Tel-Aviv residents, under fire from Arab snipers, running for cover. (The State of Israel: The National Photo Collection)

From inter-communal strife to inter-state war

In mid-December 1947, a fortnight after the outbreak of inter-communal violence, a British intelligence report estimated that 'the Arabs are beginning to succeed in making the ordinary daily round of the Jews extremely difficult. Since the beginning of the month there have been numerous attacks on communications, causing considerable concern to the community and in some cases seriously affecting their economy. This, it is thought, may possibly be the plan of the Arab Higher Committee and the Mufti – in other words, not to have a 'bloodbath', in which the Arabs would suffer from their inferior armament, but to break the economic life of the Jews and so squeeze them out of business and Palestine.'

This assessment was shared by Jewish military planners. As they saw it, the Palestinian strategy was designed to break the physical unity of the Yishuv through disruption of its land communications, thus constraining it in a number of isolated 'pockets' and undermining its ability to resist the imminent pan-Arab invasion in the wake of the forthcoming British withdrawal from Palestine.

To forestall such an eventuality the Yishuv had two possible courses of action: to occupy Arab positions controlling key roads or to vacate outlying Jewish settlements. But the former option was deemed impractical for lack of sufficient weaponry and fear of British military intervention, while the latter was precluded for political reasons, notably Ben-Gurion's conviction that any areas surrendered to the Arabs would be excluded from the territory of the nascent Jewish state in the post-war negotiations regardless of their assignment by the Partition Resolution.

These constraints had far-reaching operational implications for the Yishuv. The adoption of a defensive strategy of securing communication lines and protecting outlying settlements left the initiative in the hands of the Arabs who could determine at will where and when to launch their attacks. The decision to hang on to every single settlement substantially extended the Yishuv's lines of defence, necessitating the dispersal of forces throughout the country rather than their concentration into larger and more effective formations.

Jewish vulnerabilities

Three areas were particularly vulnerable to Arab attacks. First there were the 33 Jewish settlements to be excluded from the prospective Jewish state, which were located deep in Arab territory. Then there was the Negev, that vast and largely unpopulated desert south of the Gaza–Beersheba line, which occupied about 80 per cent of the territory assigned to the Jewish state by the Partition Resolution. The 27 isolated Jewish villages established in this area, with their tiny population of a few hundred farmers, were widely seen as an operational liability that had to be removed at the first available opportunity. Yet when some military advisers took up this matter with Ben-Gurion, they were instructed to reinforce the settlements with men and equipment. 'If we fail to defend the Negev, Tel-Aviv will not stand either,' he argued. 'If we will not be in the Negev, the [Arabs] will occupy it, and it is an illusion to think that they will subsequently return it to us.'

Last but not least was the question of Jerusalem. By virtue of geography and topography the city was the most isolated of the Yishuv's urban centres. Lying at the heart of an Arab area with only a handful of neighbouring Jewish settlements and with its

lifeline passing through hostile Arab territory, Jerusalem's Jewish population could easily be held captive to Arab war plans. To this must be added the extreme difficulty of ensuring security along the 60-kilometre-

Jewish Jerusalem's precarious geopolitical location, at the heart of an Arab area with only a handful of neighbouring Jewish settlements, allowed the Arabs to subject it to a protracted siege, resulting in severe food and water shortages. (The State of Israel: The National Photo Collection) long road between Tel-Aviv and Jerusalem, nearly half of which wound through rough and hilly country, rising up to a height of over 900 metres with frequent steep gradients and deep, narrow, tortuous defiles. All the Arabs had to do was to block the stretch of road running near their village, then sit on the overlooking ridge and aim their shots at the trapped Jewish convoys as they were busy removing the roadblocks.

To make the problem of defence still harder, the Jewish population of Jerusalem was dispersed into non-contiguous suburbs, many of them surrounded by Arab neighbourhoods. The position of the Jewish quarter of the Old City, where some 2,500 Jews were living among 22,000 Arabs, was particularly dire. Communication between this area and the rest of the Jewish

neighbourhoods in Jerusalem had been precarious even in the best of times and subject to regular disruptions by Arab mobs, especially on Muslim religious festivals. Once hostilities broke out, the quarter came under immediate siege.

It will be recalled that according to the Partition Resolution, Jerusalem was to be placed under an international régime, with its residents given the right to apply for citizenship in either the Arab or the Jewish states. The Zionist leadership, though begrudgingly acquiescing in this decision,

Car bombs constituted a popular weapon in the fighting between Palestine's Arab and Jewish communities. Here Jerusalem's Ben-Yehuda Street after a bombing in February 1948 in which 50 people were killed and hundreds wounded. (Topham Picturepoint)

had little doubt that Jerusalem would continue to play a pivotal role in the life and development of the nascent Jewish state despite its exclusion from its territory. Not only was it the holiest of sites for Judaism and Jews and the epitome of the Zionist yearning for national rebirth, but its 100,000-strong Jewish community constituted nearly one-sixth of the Yishuv's entire population. Hence, unlike the Negev and other outlying settlements, there was no doubting the need to prevent the fall of Jewish Jerusalem come what may. The cost of such an endeavour, however, was to be exorbitant given that Jewish Jerusalem was heavily dependent on outside supplies for its very survival, having no real industrial infrastructure and producing only a fraction of its food and other requirements. Indeed, more Jews would be killed in the fighting over the road to Jerusalem than in any other campaign of the 1948 War.

The Arabs on the offensive

The Arabs were quick to exploit their operational advantage. Already on the first day of the fighting, on 30 November 1947, seven people were killed in two attacks on Jewish buses to Jerusalem. On 7 December, Ben-Gurion himself ran into an Arab obstruction as he was making his way to Jerusalem for a meeting with the British High Commissioner. 'Our radiators overheated and a tire went flat,' recalled the head of Ben-Gurion's security team. 'I saw some movement on one of the hills and sent two fighters to check it out. Three men stayed with me to protect Ben-Gurion and [Moshe] Sneh (a prominent Zionist leader). As we were changing the tire, Ben-Gurion asked to get out. I told him: 'Excuse me, sir, but I am responsible for your safety. You'll sit inside, bent down'. The tire was changed. The boys sent to the hills drove away the Arabs.

Later that day, at approximately the same place, a senior Hagana commander was killed as he made his way from Jerusalem to Tel-Aviv. On 11 December, 10 Jewish fighters were killed when a convoy to Gush Etzion, a cluster of four settlements north of Hebron, was ambushed by a large Arab force. Three days later yet another relief convoy on its way to the besieged settlement of Ben-Shemen, near Lydda, was attacked by the Arab Legion. Thirteen fighters were killed, nine were seriously wounded. Another two Jewish drivers were killed when a convoy was trapped for hours in the Arab village of Yazur, south of Jaffa.

Alongside their attacks on Jewish transportation, the Arabs attempted to occupy a number of outlying settlements throughout the country. On 10 January 1948, some 900 fighters of the newly established ALA crossed the Syrian border and attacked kibbutz Kfar-Szold. Despite their overwhelming inferiority in numbers and equipment, the defenders managed to hold their ground and were eventually saved by a British armoured unit sent to their aid.

An even more ferocious attack was launched on 14 January on the Etzion Bloc. In the largest offensive in the war until then the Arabs put into battle some 1,000 men headed by Abd al-Qader al-Husseini himself. The main assault, involving a battalion of 400 trained and armed fighters, was mounted against the bloc's main settlement, Kfar-Etzion, while diversionary attacks were launched against the neighbouring kibbutzim of Masuot-Yitzhak and Ein-Zurim. So confident were the Arabs of their success that they brought with them hundreds of non-combatants, men, women and children, carrying empty bags for the loot. They were to be bitterly disappointed. Anticipating the thrust of the assault, the defenders took up concealed positions along the main route of advance, taking the attackers completely by surprise. By dusk the Arabs had retreated in disarray, leaving behind some 200 dead and a similar number of wounded, inflicted by less than 30 defenders. The large British police and military forces stationed in the neighbourhood made no attempt to stop the fighting.

Before long, however, the Arabs were to exact their revenge. With Kfar-Etzion's meagre reserves of arms and ammunition depleted in the battle, a platoon of 35 men was sent the next day to reinforce the besieged kibbutz. Commanded by Danny Mass, the Etzion Bloc's commander until a few days earlier, the group left the Jerusalem area in the evening of 15 January, but failed to reach its destination before dawn and found itself surrounded by masses of Arabs who had swarmed to the area from their villages. Taking positions near the opening of a cave on the local road, the platoon fought to the last man. A British police officer was to tell later that he found the body of one of the fighters with a stone, his last weapon, in his hand. True or not, the death of the 35 would take its place in the Israeli

The fall of the strategic village of Kastel to Hagana forces on 10 April 1948, after a week of ferocious fighting, constituted an important breakthrough in the Jewish effort to break the Arab siege around Jerusalem. (Hulton Getty)

collective memory as an epitome of heroism and in the Arab narrative as a shining military success. So much so that when the Israeli army occupied the area in the 1967 Six-Day War, many Arabs from villages who had taken part in the 1948 battle fled their homes for fear of revenge.

Five days after the Etzion Bloc battle, on 20 January, the isolated kibbutz of Yechiam, in the western Galilee, was attacked by some 400 Arab fighters armed with mortars, medium and light machine guns and rifles. The kibbutz was completely surrounded and the attack opened simultaneously from all sides. Road blocks were established at all approaches and bridges and culverts were made impassable, indicating that the attackers intended to occupy the settlement at all costs.

There being no other communication, the kibbutz managed to contact the town of Nahariya by heliograph and police armoured cars from Acre were sent out, together with a platoon of soldiers, to help the kibbutz fend off the attack. The next morning the Arabs resumed their attack with mortars and machine guns but were repelled yet again by the defenders, who had been reinforced overnight by some 60 Hagana fighters.

The attack was carried out by the 2nd Yarmuk Regiment of the ALA, which in early 1948 began penetrating Palestine in strength. Commanded by Adib al-Shishakly, a future ruler of Syria, the 2nd Regiment entered the country from Lebanon on the night of 10–11 January, setting its headquarters in the Galilean locality of Sasa. It was followed 10 days later by the 1st Yarmuk Regiment, headed by Muhammad Tzafa, which infiltrated Palestine from Transjordan. Setting his headquarters in the Samaritan town of Tubas, Tzafa dispersed his forces in the neighbouring towns of Nablus and Tulkarm as well as in local villages. Another large ALA contingent left for Palestine, via Transjordan, on the night of 28 January.

By the end of January, according to official British figures, some 3,000 ALA soldiers had infiltrated Palestine. Most of them were concentrated in the Samaria

region, where they were reconnoitring the area, collecting intelligence and seeking to assert strict military control over the local population. A month later their numbers grew to 6,000–7,000, and by mid-April they had reached 7,000–8,000. Of these 3,000–4,000 were deployed in Samaria, while another 1,000 camped in the Galilee in groups of 50–100 under a central command. A few hundred fighters were deployed in each of Palestine's primary Arab cities – Jaffa, Haifa and Jerusalem – in addition to the 500 positioned in the Jerusalem district and the 100 in the Gaza district.

The ALA's growth in strength was accompanied by a corresponding boost in self-confidence, and before long it launched its first large-scale attack on a Jewish settlement. At 3.45 am on 16 February, the 1st Yarmuk Regiment laid down a heavy barrage of mortar shells and machine gun fire on kibbutz Tirat-Zvi in the Beisan valley of the eastern Galilee. About two hours later some 300–500 troops advanced on the kibbutz with the intention of occupying it and killing its residents. They succeeded in cutting the perimeter fence at one point but failed to penetrate the inner defences, where they were in for an unpleasant surprise. Withholding their fire until the Arabs were at close range, the Jewish defenders then took the attackers completely by surprise, forcing them into a hasty retreat. Some 60 Arabs were killed in the fighting and about 100 wounded, compared to a single fatality on the Jewish side.

On the verge of defeat

In a report on the situation in Palestine, written on 23 March 1948, General Ismail Safwat, the Arab League's appointed commander of the Palestine campaign, wondered why the Jews had not used their military superiority to deal the Palestinian Arabs a mortal blow. Part of the explanation, in his opinion, lay in the Jewish belief that self-restraint was conducive to eventual Arab acquiescence in the existence of a Jewish state in line with the Partition Resolution. And the proof: 'Until now they have not attacked any Arab village unless provoked by it.' Other presumed causes of the Jewish self-restraint were the fear of British intervention, and the desire to preserve their strength for the anticipated showdown with the Arab world following the completion of the British withdrawal.

Be that as it may, at the time when the report was written the supposed Jewish prowess was nowhere to be seen. Notwithstanding a number of Jewish successes, notably the destruction of a large arms convoy from Lebanon to Haifa, the intensification of Arab attacks on Jewish transportation to Jerusalem and the Negev during the month of March led to the virtual isolation of these areas. On 24 March, a large Jewish convoy to Jerusalem was forced to turn back at the narrow ravine of Bab al-Wad (Gate of the Valley), where the coastal road sharply ascends towards Jerusalem, leaving behind 14 burned-out home-made armoured cars. Two days later, the Hagana was forced to abandon the use of the southern coastal road, which ran through densely populated Arab areas, leaving the Negev totally severed from the rest of the Yishuv. In the north, a large convoy from Haifa to the besieged settlement of Yechiam was ambushed near the Arab village of Kabri. The first few vehicles managed to break through but the rest of the convoy was trapped and all its 42 members were killed in a 10-hour battle with their attackers.

A particularly painful setback was suffered on 27 March, when a large supply convoy returning from the Etzion Bloc to Jerusalem was trapped at a roadblock south of the city. Leaving their vehicles, the men took positions inside a deserted building named after the Prophet Daniel (Nabi Daniel) from where they fought back successive assaults by thousands of armed Arabs. The battle raged for nearly 24 hours, by which time the defenders had almost run out of ammunition and had lost all hope of being reinforced. They thus agreed to be evacuated by the British army to Jerusalem, together with their cars and equipment.

In the event, the British rescued the men but surrendered their cars and weapons to the Arabs. Since the convoy included most of the Yishuv's reservoir of home-made armoured cars that had maintained communication between Tel-Aviv and Jerusalem, their loss meant the effective severance of Jerusalem from the coastal plain. And as if to underscore this bitter reality, yet another convoy that tried to break through to Jerusalem from the settlement of Hulda was ambushed and forced back after suffering a number of casualties. 'The intensification of Arab attacks on communications and particularly the failure of the Kfar Etzion convoy – probably the Yishuv's strongest armoured transport unit – to force a return passage has brought home the precarious position of Jewish communities both great and small which are dependent on supply lines running through Arab controlled country,' commented a British report. 'In particular it is now realised that the position of Jewish Jerusalem, where a food-scarcity already exists, is likely to be desperate after 16th May.'

The April turning point

By April 1948 the Jewish position seemed extremely precarious. True, for all their numerous assaults the Arabs had failed to occupy a single Jewish neighbourhood or settlement. Nor did they manage to gain the upper hand in the ongoing fighting in Palestine's main urban centres, Jaffa, Haifa and Jerusalem. Yet the Yishuv was beginning to reel from the war's heavy human and material cost. According to official British figures, by early April 1948, Jewish casualties had amounted to 875 dead and 1,858 wounded, compared with 967 and 1,911 Arab casualties respectively. Given that the Yishuv's population was roughly half the size of its Arab counterpart, these losses were proportionately twice as heavy as those suffered by the latter.

Major-General Hugh Stockwell, Commander of the British forces in northern Palestine, tried to mediate a truce agreement between the Arab and Jewish communities in Haifa. The Arabs refused to sign the agreement and evacuated the remaining Arab population from the city. (Topham Picturepoint)

The impact of this human toll was further exacerbated by the setbacks of late March. There were manifestations of declining morale and growing disorientation and doubts were voiced about the Yishuv's ability to weather the storm. Most alarmingly, given the tight siege around Jewish Jerusalem and the attendant shortages in basic commodities, as well as in weapons and ammunition, the possibility of the city's fall could no longer be precluded unless some dramatic action was immediately taken. 'It is becoming increasingly apparent that the Yishuv and its leaders are deeply worried about the future,' read a British report. 'The 100,000 Jews of Jerusalem have been held to ransom and it is doubtful whether the Arab economic blockade of the city can be broken by Jewish forces alone. If the Jewish leaders are not prepared to sacrifice the 100,000 Jews of Jerusalem, then they must concede, however unwillingly, that the Arabs have won the second round in the struggle which began with a Jewish victory in the first round on the 29th November.'

To make things worse, the US administration seemed to be backtracking from its earlier support for partition. The creation of a Jewish state had always been anathema to American foreign policy and defence department officials. Reluctant to alienate the oil-rich and strategically located Arab states and apprehensive of the possibility of having to send American troops to the rescue of the nascent Jewish state were it to be overwhelmed by its Arab neighbours, they had done their utmost to abort the partition of Palestine, only to be overruled by President Harry Truman. Now that the Palestinian Arabs seemed to be gaining the upper hand, even without the interference of the Arab states, the bureaucrats managed to have their way. On 19 March 1948, the United States representative to the UN, Warren Austin, announced that since the conflict in Palestine had proved that partition was no longer possible, the country should be placed under a UN trusteeship.

In these circumstances, an early operational breakthrough became, literally, a matter of life and death for the Yishuv. Already in mid-March, the Hagana adopted a new strategic plan, code named Plan D, as the framework for all operational planning. Unlike its defensive precursors, plans A, B and C, which had hitherto dominated the Hagana's strategic thought, Plan D sought to turn the tables on the Arabs by seizing the operational initiative. Taking for granted a pan-Arab invasion that would seek to severe and/or occupy substantial parts of Palestine, and the consequent need for ensuring territorial continuity and depth in the areas under Jewish control already before the invasion began, the plan aimed at 'gaining control over the territory assigned to the Jewish state and defending its borders, as well as the blocs of Jewish settlement and such Jewish population as were outside those borders, against regular, para-regular, and guerrilla forces operating from bases outside or inside the nascent Jewish state'. To achieve these objectives, Plan D outlined a mixture of static and mobile operational measures, including counter-attacks on enemy bases and communications lines,

both within Palestine and in the neighbouring Arab states; the capture of key roads to ensure the freedom of movement for military and economic purposes; the occupation of forward bases on enemy territory to deny their use as a springboard for an attack on the Jewish state; economic pressure on the Palestinian Arabs so as to force them to cease hostilities; the capture of certain Palestinian towns and villages in order to undermine their guerrilla campaign; and the seizure of government institutions and assets following the British withdrawal with a view to ensuring the functioning of key public services. In a message to his commanders, the Hagana's chief of staff, Israel Galili, took great pains to clarify that 'the behaviour of the *Hagana* towards the Arabs in the territory of the Hebrew state, or in predominantly Jewish areas containing Arab enclaves, stems from the Arab policy of the Zionist Movement, that is, acknowledgement of the full rights, needs, and freedom of the Arabs in the Hebrew state without any discrimination, and a desire for co-existence on the basis of mutual freedom and dignity'.

In line with this plan, it was decided on 1 April to breach the Arab siege of Jerusalem by securing a corridor on both sides of the Tel-Aviv–Jerusalem road, ranging in width from six miles in the coastal plain to two in the mountains. Operation Nachshon, as it was code-named, was to be the Hagana's debut as a conventional military force. Until then, its operations had never been above the company level. Now, at Ben-Gurion's insistence, a brigade-sized operation was to be mounted, involving some 1,500 fighters organised in three battalions. This in turn necessitated the dilution of Jewish forces throughout the country, but Ben-Gurion saw no other alternative. 'If Jerusalem falls, the whole country might fall,' he warned his commanders as they were deliberating the operation. 'The risk is worth taking. This is the hinge on which everything rests.'

Launched on 6 April, Operation Nachshon was preceded by two subsidiary local actions. The first was the capture, on

The fall of Hafia on 21–22 April 1948 led to general disorientation among the Palestinian Arabs and to the surrender of many of the country's foremost Arab cities. On 11 May Safed fell to the Hagana and Jaffa followed suit a couple of days later. (The State of Israel: The National Photo Collection)

the night of 2–3 April, of the strategic village of Kastel dominating the approaches to Jerusalem about five miles to the west of the city. The second, and no less important, was the blowing up of Hasan Salame's headquarters in the town of Ramle in the early morning of 5 April. The destruction of this heavily fortified and guarded base in which some 30 Arab fighters were killed dealt a powerful blow to Salame's prestige and prevented his forces from playing an active role in the fighting over the Jerusalem road. By 15 April, when Operation Nachshon came to an end, the Jewish forces had managed to occupy a number of Arab villages along the Tel-Aviv–Jerusalem road and to get three large convoys with food and weapons to Jerusalem.

Fighting was particularly intense around the Kastel, which changed hands several times until 10 April when the Arab forces finally withdrew following the death of their commander, Abd al-Qader al-Husseini. The implications of this death for the Palestinian national struggle extended well beyond the fall of the strategic village. It led to a widespread loss of purpose and demoralisation, with thousands of mourners participating in the funeral. In an ironic twist of history, the person who had been quite controversial during his lifetime, whose military record had been far from a success story and whose recruitment efforts had been spurned by numerous villages and towns (two months before his death Abd al-Qader was widely ridiculed in local coffee houses as 'Corporal Qader') had been instantaneously transformed into a national hero by virtue of his death.

A further blow to Arab morale was dealt on 9 April, the day after Abd al-Qader's death, when Irgun and Lehi fighters occupied the village of Deir Yasin, on the outskirts of Jerusalem, killing in the process some 100 people (the figure given at the time was more than twice as high), including many women and children. Although the Irgun categorically denied any massacres, claiming that the casualties had been caused in the course of heavy fighting; although the

Jewish Agency and the Hagana immediately expressed their deep disgust and regret; and while the Arabs swiftly exacted their revenge by killing some 80 Jewish nurses and doctors en route to the Haddasah hospital on Mount Scopus, Arab propaganda quickly capitalised on the tragedy in an attempt to reap immediate political gains. In the long run, Deir Yasin would indeed become the most effective Arab propaganda tool against Israel. At the time, however, the widely exaggerated descriptions of Jewish atrocities, especially the alleged rapes of women that had never taken place, spread panic in the Palestinian public and intensified the ongoing mass flight from the country.

No less detrimental to the Palestinian war effort was the abortive attempt by the ALA to occupy the settlement of Mishmar-Haemek in the western Galilee. Reeling from the humiliating defeat at Tirat-Zvi, al-Qawuqji viewed the Hagana's preoccupation with Operation Nachshon as an opportunity to prove the ALA's mettle. The choice of Mishmar-Haemek could not have been better from a military point of view. Lying at the foothills of Mount Ephraim, opposite the Jezreel valley, the kibbutz was overlooked by a number of Arab villages and flanked by some others. Its occupation would have allowed the Arabs to isolate the strategic town of Haifa by blocking the Wadi Milleh valley, through which all Jewish traffic between Tel-Aviv and Haifa had to pass following the closure of the country's main south–north artery along the Mediterranean, to Jewish transportation.

In the early hours of 4 April, the ALA landed a heavy artillery barrage on Mishmar-Haemek using seven field guns it had received from Syria. This was followed by an attack by some 1,000 soldiers which was contained by the defenders at the village perimeter. A second attack, the next day, was stopped by the British, who mediated a 24-hour ceasefire for the evacuation of women, children and wounded from the kibbutz. When fighting was resumed, the Jews seized the initiative. An infantry battalion, led by the Palmach's founding father, Yitzhak Sadeh, counter-attacked and captured several Arab villages and strongholds in the mountains above and in the rear of the kibbutz. For the next five days and nights the two sides would battle over these sites, with the Jews taking them by night and the Arabs using their numerical and material superiority to regain them the following day; one stronghold was subjected to no less than 11 consecutive Arab attacks.

In growing desperation on 12 April al-Qawuqji mounted yet another large assault on Mishmar-Haemek, only to find his forces routed and in danger of encirclement. Realising that all was lost, he ordered a hasty withdrawal to the town of Jenin, in the Samaria area. Meanwhile, Hagana forces defeated an attack by a Druze battalion on kibbutz Ramat-Yohanan, north of Mishmar-Haemek, aimed at relieving the pressure from the ALA. The Jewish position in the south-western Galilee had been secured.

The fall of the Arab cities

Encouraged by its recent operational successes, the Hagana pressed ahead with the implementation of Plan D, by seeking to gain control over the 'mixed' towns and cities in the nascent Jewish state. On 18 April Jewish forces captured the town of Tiberias, overlooking the Sea of Galilee, where some 6,500 Jews and 2,000 Arabs were living. Ignoring the pleas of the local Jewish leadership, the Arabs chose to leave the town *en masse* and were vacated by the British army. The same scenario was to repeat itself within days, albeit on a far wider scale, in the city of Haifa, home to 75,000 Jews and 62,500 Arabs.

From the outbreak of Arab–Jewish hostilities, Haifa became engulfed in intermittent violence that pitted Arab fighters, recruited locally as well as from neighbouring Arab countries, against the Hagana. The hostilities would reach their peak on 21–22 April 1948, when the British suddenly decided to evacuate most of the town and each of the two parties moved in

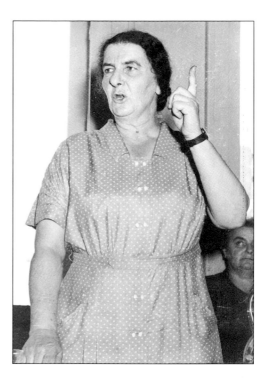

On 11 May 1948 the Acting Head of the Jewish Agency's Political Department, Golda Meir, held a secret meeting with Transjordan's King Abdallah in an abortive attempt to prevent the imminent pan-Arab invasion. (Topham Picturepoint)

quickly to try to fill the vacuum and assert control. By this time, only about half of Haifa's original Arab community remained, the rest having fled the town in the preceding months.

But not for long. Disheartened by the desertion of their local military leaders, and petrified by wildly exaggerated accounts of the Deir Yasin tragedy, the remnant now took to the road. In the early morning of 22 April, as Hagana forces battled their way to the downtown market area, thousands streamed into the port, still held by the British army. Within hours, many of these had fled by trains and buses, while the rest awaited evacuation by sea.

What was left of the local Arab leadership now asked the British military to stop the fighting. When this failed, a delegation requested a meeting with the British commander, Major-General Hugh Stockwell,

The Battle for Haifa

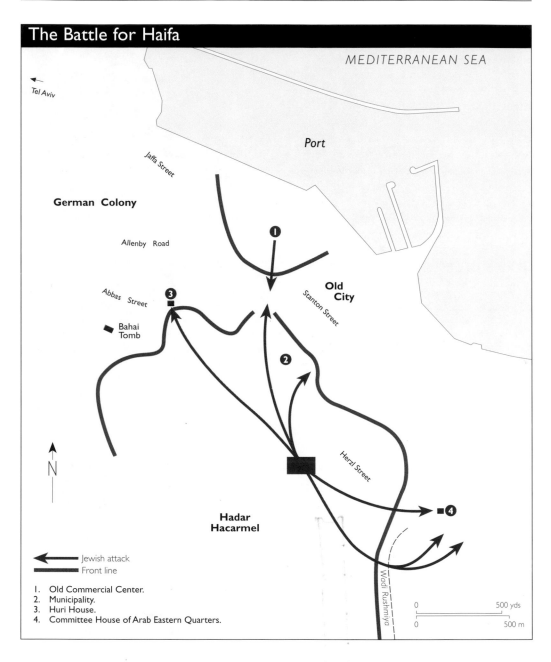

MEDITERRANEAN SEA

Tel Aviv

Port

Jaffa Street

German Colony

Allenby Road

Abbas Street

3

Bahai
Tomb

Old
City

Stanton Street

2

Herzl Street

N

**Hadar
Hacarmel**

Wadi Rushmiya

4

Jewish attack
Front line

1. Old Commercial Center.
2. Municipality.
3. Huri House.
4. Committee House of Arab Eastern Quarters.

0   500 yds
0   500 m

'with a view to obtaining a truce with the Jews'. Having learned from Stockwell the Hagana's terms for such a truce, the delegates then left to consult with their peers, before meeting their Jewish counterparts at 4.00 pm at City Hall.

There, after an impassioned plea for peace and reconciliation by the town's Jewish mayor, Shabtai Levy, the assembled delegates went through the truce terms point by point,

modifying a number of them to meet Arab objections. Then the Arabs requested a 24-hour recess 'to give them the opportunity to contact their brothers in the Arab states'. Although this was deemed unacceptable, a brief break was approved and the meeting adjourned at 5.20 pm. When the Arabs returned that evening at 7.15 pm, they had a surprise in store: as Stockwell would later put it in his official report, they stated 'that they were not in a position to sign the truce, as they had no control over the Arab military elements in the town and that, in all sincerity, they could not fulfil the terms of the truce, even if they were to sign'. They then offered, 'as an alternative, that the Arab population wished to evacuate Haifa and that they would be grateful for military assistance'. This came as a bombshell. With tears in his eyes, the elderly Levy pleaded with the Arabs, most of whom were his personal acquaintances, to reconsider, saying that they were committing 'a cruel crime against their own people'. Yaacov Salomon, a prominent Haifa lawyer and the Hagana's chief liaison officer in the city, followed suit, assuring the Arab delegates that he 'had the instructions of the commander of the zone ... that if they stayed on they would enjoy equality and peace, and that we, the Jews, were interested in their staying on and the maintenance of harmonious relations'. Even the stoic Stockwell was shaken. 'You have made a foolish decision,' he thundered at

the Arabs. 'Think it over, as you'll regret it afterward. You must accept the conditions of the Jews. They are fair enough. Don't permit life to be destroyed senselessly. After all, it was you who began the fighting, and the Jews have won.'

But the Arabs were unmoved. The next morning, they met with Stockwell and his advisers to discuss the practicalities of the evacuation. Of the 30,000+ Arabs still in Haifa, only a handful, they said, wished to stay. Perhaps the British could provide 80 trucks a day and in the meantime ensure an orderly supply of foodstuffs in the city and its environs? At this, a senior British officer at the meeting erupted: 'If you sign your truce you would automatically get all your food worries over. You are merely starving your own people.' 'We will not sign,' the Arabs retorted. 'All is already lost, and it does not matter if everyone is killed so

The battle for Palestine. Israeli Forces capture Beersheba, 2 November 1948. (Topham Picturepoint)

While Golda Meir was meeting with Abdallah, the Arab Legion was battering the Etzion Bloc, a cluster of four Jewish settlements north of Hebron. (Topham Picturepoint)

long as we do not sign the document.' Within a matter of days, only about 3,000 of Haifa's Arab residents remained in the city.

What had produced the seemingly instantaneous sea change from explicit interest in a truce to its rejection only a few hours later? It later transpired that during the brief respite in the negotiations granted to them, the Arab delegates proceeded to telephone the AHC office in Beirut for instructions. They were then told explicitly not to sign, but instead to evacuate the town. Astonished, the Haifa delegates protested but were assured that 'it is only a matter of days' before Arab retaliatory action would commence, and 'since there will be a lot of casualties following our intended action ... you [would] be held responsible for the casualties among the Arab population left in the town'. Reluctant to shoulder this heavy burden, the startled delegation returned to City Hall to announce its decision to vacate Haifa's Arab populace.

The implications of this development cannot be overstated. Haifa was no ordinary local town but one of Palestine's foremost socio-political and administrative centres for both Arabs and Jews. It was one of the primary ports of the eastern Mediterranean, the hub of Palestine's railway system, the site of the country's oil refinery and a formidable industrial centre. Its Arab population was second in size only to that of Jaffa, accounting for one-tenth of the total Palestinian dispersion. Little wonder, then, that the fall of Haifa had a devastating impact on Palestinian morale, accelerating their collapse and flight in numerous locations throughout the country. On 11 May, Safed fell to the Jews, followed the next day by Beisan. On 13 May, the town of Jaffa, allocated to the Arab state by the Partition Resolution, surrendered to the Hagana, with the remaining population dispersing en masse.

No less importantly, the fall of Haifa gave the final spur to the Arab states' decision to invade Palestine. As Abd al-Rahman Azzam, secretary-general of the Arab League, declared shortly after the event: 'The Zionists are seizing the opportunity to establish a Zionist state against the will of the Arabs. The Arab peoples have accepted the challenge and soon they will close their account with them.'

On the eve of invasion

By mid-May, the war effort of the Palestinian Arabs had all but collapsed. Their foremost military leaders had either been killed (notably Abd al-Qader al-Husseini) or discredited (Hasan Salame), with their forces thrown into disarray. The ALA was smarting from the Mishmar-Haemek defeat. Four of the six mixed towns – Haifa, Jaffa, Safed and Tiberias – were in Jewish hands, while Acre had been isolated. Only in Jerusalem did the Arabs hold their ground and even there a mass flight from many neighbourhoods took place. Some 100 Arab villages throughout the country had been deserted by their inhabitants or captured by the Hagana, which by now had re-opened the main road arteries in the north and south of the country to Jewish transportation. About 200,000 Palestinians had fled their homes, many of them to the neighbouring Arab states.

For its part the Yishuv remained wary of the formidable obstacles that lay ahead. 'We are still far away from the required force to meet 15th May,' Ben-Gurion told a high-level meeting on 16 April 1948. 'We lack almost half of the necessary manpower, about 80 per cent of the vehicles, and substantial additional equipment.'

On 7 May, a week before the termination of the British Mandate, Ben-Gurion was still concerned. After a sustained mobilisation drive, begun in the wake of the UN partition vote, the Hagana had mustered some 29,900 members: 16,400 field fighters organised in nine brigades and 13,500 settlers defending their villagers and towns. Yet only 60 per cent of the fighters were armed (for example, 1,200 of 2,200 fighters in the Alexandroni Brigade and 1,200 of 2,000 in the Givati Brigade) and there were serious shortages in explosives, ammunition and vehicles.

In a last-ditch attempt to prevent an Arab invasion, Ben-Gurion sent Golda Meir, Acting Head of the Jewish Agency's Political Department, on a secret mission to King Abdallah, who in early May was made commander-in-chief of the impending pan-Arab campaign. The two had already met secretly on 17 November 1947, but had failed to reach an agreement due to Abdallah's desire to annex the whole of Palestine, or at least its Arab parts, to his kingdom, and Meir's insistence on a two-state solution in accordance with UNSCOP majority recommendations. In their second meeting, on 11 May 1948, the king was no more receptive to the idea of Jewish statehood. 'Why are you in such a hurry to proclaim your state?,' he asked. 'Why don't you wait a few years? I will take over the whole country and you will be represented in my parliament. I will treat you very well and there will be no war.' Meir's categorical rejection of the idea failed to impress the king. Even as she was taking her leave, Abdallah reiterated his request to

consider his offer, 'and if the reply were affirmative, it had to be given before 15 May'.

As the king was meeting with Mrs Meir, his Arab Legion was battering the Etzion Bloc. The attack began on 4 May, when a Legion unit, assisted by Arab irregulars from the neighbouring villages and a number of British tanks, tried to seize high ground in the midst of the bloc so as to split it in half. This was achieved within a week and on 13 May the Legion stormed the bloc's main kibbutz, Kfar-Etzion. Fifteen defenders, who had laid down their weapons, were summarily slaughtered, together with dozens of other defenders and civilians, including an Arab family who had been living on the kibbutz. Only three men and a girl survived to tell the story. The bloc's other three

At four o'clock on the afternoon of 14 May 1948 the Chairman of the Jewish Agency, David Ben-Gurion, proclaimed the State of Israel. A few hours later the newly established state was attacked by five Arab armies. (The State of Israel: The National Photo Collection)

The invading Syrian forces managed to occupy a number of Israeli settlements, but were beaten back at Degania, the first kibbutz to have been established. Here a damaged Syrian tank outside Degania. (The State of Israel: The National Photo Collection)

kibbutzim surrendered the next day, following mediation by the International Red Cross, and were taken prisoners by the Legion.

The fall of the Etzion Bloc, together with Meir's failed mission, provided the final proof, if such were needed at all at this stage, of the inevitability of an Arab invasion. At four o'clock on the afternoon of 14 May 1948 Ben-Gurion proclaimed the establishment of the State of Israel, becoming its first Prime Minister and Minister of Defence. That night the armies of five Arab states attacked the newly created state.

From invasion to first truce

According to the invasion plan, agreed by the Arab leaders in late April, the Syrian,

Lebanese, Iraqi and Transjordanian armies were to invade the nascent Jewish state from all directions in a wide pincer movement aimed at occupying the Galilee and the eastern Jezreel valley before reaching their main objective, the port town of Haifa. Meanwhile the Egyptian army would advance on Tel-Aviv, thus occupying the country's southern part and diverting maximum Israeli forces from the Arab assault on Haifa.

Though this plan had never been fully implemented, owing to mutual Arab distrust and the consequent lack of adequate operational co-operation, the simultaneous invasion of Israel stretched to the limit the Jewish geostrategic vulnerabilities that had

OPPOSITE TOP: The capture of Jerusalem constituted King Abdallah's foremost political-strategic objective during the war. Here the city's Jewish Quarter under Arab Legion fire. (Topham Picturepoint)

OPPOSITE BOTTOM: As a second truce was about to go into effect on 18 July 1948, the Israeli army managed to capture the strategic towns of Lydda and Ramle on the central front. (Topham Picturepoint)

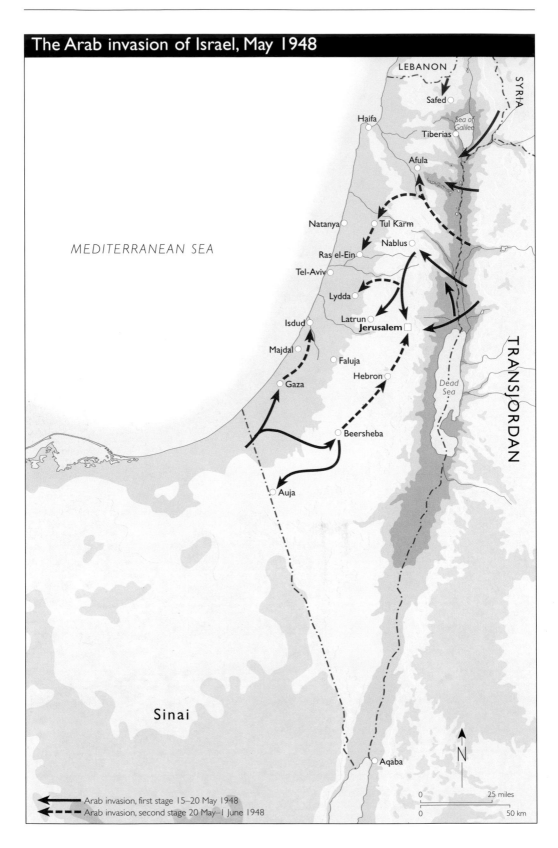

The Arab invasion of Israel, May 1948

LEBANON

SYRIA

Safed

Haifa

Sea of Galilee

Tiberias

Afula

Natanya

Tul Karm

Nablus

MEDITERRANEAN SEA

Ras el-Ein

Tel-Aviv

Lydda

Latrun

Jerusalem

Isdud

Majdal

Faluja

Hebron

Dead Sea

Gaza

TRANSJORDAN

Beersheba

Auja

Sinai

Aqaba

N

0   25 miles

0   50 km

→ Arab invasion, first stage 15–20 May 1948

→ Arab invasion, second stage 20 May–1 June 1948

From the earliest days of the war the Arabs sought to exploit their control of Palestine's main road arteries to attack Jewish transportation throughout the country. The Hagana sought to overcome this predicament by arranging large convoys to strategic locations. Here a convoy arriving in Jerusalem. (Topham Picturepoint)

already been revealed during the war with the Palestinians. Many Jewish settlements, especially in the Galilee and the Negev, found themselves totally isolated and were forced to rely on their own tenacity and meagre resources (for example, 22 of the Negev's 27 settlements had fewer than 30 defenders).

In an attempt to incorporate its diverse underground organisations into a unified national force, on 28 May the provisional government issued the Israel Defence Forces (IDF) Establishment Order. The Hagana's general staff and commanders continued their functions at the newly established army, while the Irgun and Lehi were disbanded and their members were absorbed into the IDF (only in Jerusalem, which had not yet been incorporated into the nascent State of Israel, did the two organisations continue their activities until September 1948, when they were finally disbanded).

The invading Egyptian force consisted of some 6,000 troops, organised in two infantry brigades and a number of independent battalions, and assisted by some 2,000 Egyptian irregulars, mainly from the militant religious organisation the Muslim Brothers, who had been operating in Palestine for some time. Springing from positions in the eastern part of the Sinai Peninsula, which it had taken in late April, the Egyptian contingent mounted a three-pronged assault: one formation advanced along the coastal road towards Tel-Aviv, another was landed by ship at Majdal, north of Gaza, while a third force moved north-east of Beersheba with some of its units proceeding as far as the outskirts of Jerusalem, where they linked up with Transjordan's Arab Legion.

In order to protect their rear, the Egyptians sought to occupy a number of northern Negev kibbutzim. The first to come under attack was Kfar-Darom, a religious kibbutz some 10 kilometres south of Gaza, which had already withstood an assault by Muslim Brothers fighters. After an artillery barrage, eight tanks approached the kibbutz, followed by infantry, only to beat a hasty retreat after

taking direct hits from the kibbutz's only Piat anti-tank weapon. The story repeated itself in the neighbouring kibbutz of Nirim, where the 40-odd defenders managed to contain sustained Egyptian assaults backed by air bombardment.

The only kibbutz the Egyptians managed to occupy at that stage was Yad-Moerdechai, whose fate was sealed by virtue of its strategic location on the coastal road

between Gaza and Tel-Aviv. Having meticulously prepared the attack, the Egyptians threw to battle an entire brigade comprising two infantry battalions, an armoured battalion and an artillery regiment. The 100 defenders managed to hold their ground for five days, by which time many of them had been wounded or killed and their ammunition nearly depleted. On 24 May, under cover of darkness, their

remnants abandoned the kibbutz, creeping through enemy lines and carrying their wounded with them. Yet the kibbutz's dogged resistance gave the IDF a much needed respite to reinforce its forces south of

On 14 May 1948 the British High Commissioner for Palestine, General Sir Alan Cunningham, left the country, bringing to an end three decades of British mandatory rule. (Hulton Getty)

Tel-Aviv and to absorb some heavier weapons and fighter aircraft that had been purchased prior to 14 May but prevented from arriving in the country by the British naval blockade. Consequently, the Egyptian

In order to protect their rear and flanks, the invading Egyptian forces sought to occupy a number of Israeli settlements in the northern Negev. After five days of heavy fighting they managed to capture the strategically located kibbutz of Yad Mordechai. (The State of Israel: The National Photo Collection)

The situation after the first truce, 11 June 1948

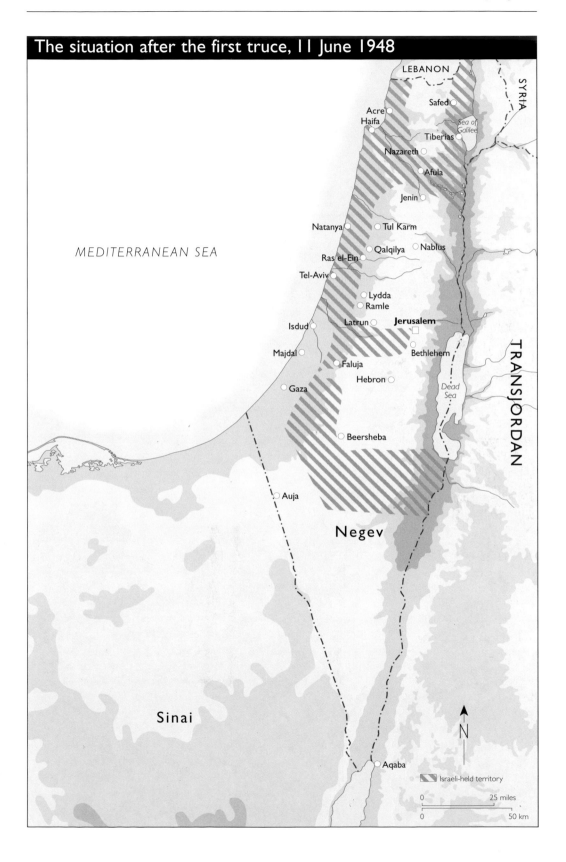

LEBANON

SYRIA

Acre

Safed

Haifa

Sea of Galilee

Tiberias

Nazareth

Afula

Jenin

Natanya

Tul Karm

Qalqilya

Nablus

Ras el-Ein

Tel-Aviv

MEDITERRANEAN SEA

Lydda

Ramle

Latrun

Jerusalem

Isdud

Bethlehem

Majdal

TRANSJORDAN

Faluja

Hebron

Dead Sea

Gaza

Beersheba

Auja

Negev

Sinai

N

Aqaba

Israeli-held territory

0   25 miles

0   50 km

column advancing on Tel-Aviv stopped some 30 kilometres south of the city, where it dug in and spent the next weeks in intermittent exchanges and sporadic attacks on local kibbutzim. For its part, the IDF failed in its attempt to breach the Egyptian siege of the Negev by capturing the police fort at the village of Iraq Sueidan, near Majdal.

Meanwhile as the Egyptians were moving towards Tel-Aviv and Jerusalem, the IDF were busy containing Arab attacks on other fronts. Having suffered some painful blows while fighting in the upper Jordan valley, an Iraqi division comprising one armoured and two infantry brigades, took up positions in the Samaria area known as the 'triangle', between the towns of Nablus, Jenin and Tulkarm, from where on 25 May it launched an attack in the direction of Netanya. This failed, but the IDF was sufficiently alarmed by the prospect of yet another thrust by this formidable force towards the coastal plain – which could, if successful, cut through the Jewish state – as to launch on 29 May a counter-attack aimed at establishing defensive positions vis-à-vis the Iraqi contingent. An Israeli force even managed to occupy Jenin, but was dislodged from the town after three days of heavy fighting with the Iraqis. Thereafter the status quo between the Israeli and the Iraqi forces was retained until the declaration of the first truce on 11 June 1948. The only Iraqi gain prior to the truce was the occupation of the headwaters of the Yarkon River and the pumping station at Ras el-Ein, some 20 kilometres south-east of Tel Aviv, which provided the water to Jerusalem.

North of the Iraqis, a Syrian infantry brigade, together with a mechanised battalion, an artillery regiment, and a company of tanks, crossed into Israel on the night of 15 May with a view to storming the cluster of kibbutzim around the Sea of Galilee before forging ahead into the central Galilee and Haifa. This did not happen as the kibbutzim held their ground for much longer than anticipated. It was only on 18 May that the Syrians managed to capture kibbutz Zemakh, at the southern tip of the Sea of Galilee and force the evacuation of

two neighbouring kibbutzim. Yet following their failure to occupy Degania, the first kibbutz to have been established (in 1909), they withdrew from Zemakh and redeployed in the hills to the east. Their only lasting achievement was the occupation on 10 June of kibbutz Mishmar-Hayarden, a day before the first truce came into effect.

The Lebanese Army was only marginally more successful. On 15 May, it managed to capture the village of Malkiya, the eastern gateway from Lebanon to Israel, only to lose it three days later to an Israeli counter-attack. On 6 June, a combined two-brigade force of the Syrian, Lebanese and ALA troops attacked and re-occupied Malkiya, thus allowing the ALA to redeploy and consolidate its forces in the Arab-populated central Galilee.

The war for Jerusalem

In a telegram to the British Foreign Office on 13 April, Sir Alec Kirkbride, the influential British ambassador to Amman, reported that the Transjordanian Government 'realised that Jerusalem presents too big a problem for the Arab Legion to deal with alone, [hence] present intention is to avoid a clash with the Jews but whether or not this will be possible remains to be seen'.

Reality, however, was quite different. Far from presenting 'too big a problem', Jerusalem constituted one of King Abdallah's foremost political–strategic objectives. An astute politician, Abdallah was keenly aware of the enormous prestige attending the inclusion of Jerusalem in his kingdom, not least in view of the Hashemites' loss in the 1920s of their historic custodianship of Islam's holiest shrines in Mecca and Medina to their nemesis, the House of Saud. Ignoring the discrepancy between this ambition and those of the Palestinians and the Arab states, not to mention the Partition Resolution, he began to put his strategy in place even before the termination of the Mandate by occupying then destroying the Etzion Bloc. Once the British were out and his hands were free, Abdallah ordered the Legion into Jerusalem.

This development could not have been more inauspicious for the Israelis. On 20 April, the newly established Harel Brigade, commanded by Yitzhak Rabin and which had secured the corridor to Jerusalem, opened during Operation Nachshon, was ordered to the city and the ALA immediately seized the high ground dominating the road to the city. Recognising its mistake, on 8 May the Hagana mounted a new offensive, code-named Operation Maccabee, to recapture these sites. For the next 10 days, forces from the Harel and the Givati brigades were to be locked in bitter fighting with the ALA, with positions changing hands several times. By 14 May, Givati had occupied a number of strategic strongholds, including the ancient fortress of Gezer, south of the Tel-Aviv–Jerusalem road, only to see victory snatched from its fingers as it was transferred to the south to contain the Egyptian invasion. Fortunately for the Israelis, owing to a series of misunderstandings between the ALA and the Arab Legion, the former had vacated its positions, including the police fortress of Latrun dominating the road, before the latter moved in. And so, on 16 May, the road to Jewish Jerusalem was open again, though this was not for long. Now it was the Israelis' turn to be negligent and to leave the Latrun stronghold unmanned. This vacuum was quickly filled by the Arab Legion, whose British commander, Sir John Bagot Glubb, or Glubb Pasha as he was commonly known, quickly recognised Latrun's vital strategic importance and did not fail to seize the golden opportunity given to him. Jewish Jerusalem was besieged again.

As the last British forces left Jerusalem on 14 May, the Jews and the Arabs rushed to fill

One of the main successes of Operation Yoav was the capture of the central Negev town of Beersheba. (The State of Israel: The National Photo Collection)

the vacuum. Two days later the Hagana had consolidated its control over the Jewish neighbourhoods in west Jerusalem but was forced to vacate the outlying neighbourhoods of Atarot and Neve-Yaacov in the north of the city. The Jewish community of the Old City was still besieged, while kibbutz Ramat-Rahel, in the south of the city, came under a ferocious attack on 21 May by a joint force of the Arab Legion and the Muslim Brothers. For the next four days the place was to change hands several times until it was recaptured on 25 May by the defenders, assisted by forces from the Harel Brigade, never to fall again.

By this time the Arab Legion had subjected the whole of Jewish Jerusalem to a sustained assault, with more than 10,000 artillery and mortar shells raining day and night on the city. Food, water and fuel were in extremely short supply. Since the water pipeline from the coast had been blown up, each family was rationed one bucket of water, obtained from wells and cisterns. Weeds from gardens and open spaces were collected and cooked over open fires for lack of food, fuel and electricity. Cemeteries were inaccessible because of the heavy fighting and people were buried where they fell, in back gardens. Still Jewish Jerusalem held its ground, repelling successive penetration attempts by the Arab Legion, often in hand-to-hand fighting. The Old City's Jewish Quarter was the only Jewish neighbourhood to succumb to the Legion's attacks: on 28 May, with only 36 of its 300 fighters capable of manning positions, and with hardly any ammunition left, the local commander gave the surrender order.

In the meantime the Hagana had been seeking to break the siege of Jerusalem by recapturing Latrun. To this end, a special formation, the 7th Brigade, was hastily assembled and thrown into battle within a week of its formation, without being given a chance to organise or train properly. The results, not surprisingly, were little short of catastrophic. Facing the best-trained Arab army, sheltered in heavily fortified positions, and having lost the element of surprise owing to navigation problems, the brigade

OPPOSITE: An Israeli soldier with a local Arab resident in Majdal, after the town's capture by the IDF. (The State of Israel: The National Photo Collection)

made its first assault together with units from the Alexandroni Brigade, at dawn of 25 May, in full view of enemy forces. A withdrawal was promptly ordered, during which the Jewish forces suffered hundreds of casualties.

Notwithstanding this painful defeat, and the critical situation throughout the country, Ben-Gurion remained adamant on Jerusalem's immediate relief. A second assault on Latrun was thus hatched on 30 May. This time the attackers managed to penetrate into the compound's courtyard, but failed to breach the fortress's wall and were forced to withdraw. Yet another attack on the night of 9–10 June was similarly stillborn.

Fortunately for Israel, an alternative route between Jerusalem and the coast was found. Dubbed the Burma Road, it was a rough dirt track broken by a stiff wadi, and made fit for vehicles in a short period of time. And so, by the time the first truce went into effect on 11 June, Jewish Jerusalem could be resupplied again, however tenuously, just as it was down to its last food rations.

From truce to truce

The truce could not have been more timely for both sides. With its human resources extended to the limit, and its war matériel markedly inferior to that of its Arab adversaries, Israel needed a respite to regroup, reorganise and absorb the weapons systems that were being shipped from Europe and the United States. For their part, after a month of fighting, the Arabs had failed to achieve their overarching goal of nipping the nascent Jewish state in the bud, with only a few Israeli settlements falling into their hands. Most of their armies were in desperate need for reorganisation and replenishment, especially the Arab Legion, which had taken heavy casualties and suffered from an acute ammunition shortage.

The war had also exposed the depth of inter-Arab enmities and reluctance to subordinate self-interest to the Arab collective good. Egypt, for one, confiscated a large shipment of ammunition, sent from the British military stores in the Canal Zone and intended for the Arab Legion.

Little wonder therefore that both Arabs and Israelis used the lull in the fighting to improve their respective positions, in total disregard of the truce's prerequisite to freeze the military situation as it had existed prior to its entry in force. When hostilities ceased on 11 June, there were some 60,000 active combatants – Arabs and Jews – in Palestine; when they were resumed on 8 July, these forces had expanded to about 100,000. Even more striking was the shift in the material balance of forces. At the time of the truce, the British believed that 'the Jews are too weak in armament to achieve spectacular success', as the fledgling IDF was beset by acute shortages of small arms, not to speak of major weapons systems that could confront the deadly Arab arsenal of aircraft, tanks, artillery and armoured cars. When fighting resumed, Israel had a number of aircraft, tanks and artillery, as well as numerous mortars and sufficient small arms. This in turn allowed it to seize the initiative and move on to the offensive.

On 9 July, the IDF attacked the Syrian positions near Mishmar-Hayarden in an attempt to push them back across the Jordan River. This failed, but yet another offensive, codenamed Operation Dekel, managed to capture a string of villages and towns, notably Nazareth, thus bringing the Lower Galilee, from Haifa Bay to the Sea of Galilee, under Israeli control.

In the south the IDF moved quickly to contain the Egyptians, who on the morning of 8 July launched a series of attacks in an attempt to consolidate their blockade of the Negev, and for the next eight days conducted heavy battles with the Egyptian forces. On the night of 17 July, with another truce looming, the IDF managed to breach the Egyptian line and to open a tenuous corridor to the isolated Negev settlements.

But the main IDF offensive during this period was directed against the Arab Legion, in an attempt to occupy the strategic towns of Ramle and Lydda, assigned by the UN to the Arab state, before moving against Latrun and Ramallah with a view to breaking the siege of Jerusalem. Codenamed Operation Danny and headed by Yigal Allon, the commander of the Palmach, the Israeli force advanced in a pincer movement, simultaneously closing on the towns from the north-west and the south-west. Having seized a dozen neighbouring villages, on 11 July it occupied Lydda and its 30,000-strong population, many of them refugees from other parts of the country, either fled or were herded on to the road of Ramallah. The next day Ramle surrendered after a brief engagement and, north of this sector, the vital springs of Ras el-Ein, which had been seized by the Iraqis in June, were recaptured. Only in Latrun did the Arab Legion hold its ground against the Israeli offensive.

When a second UN-organised truce went into effect on 18 July, Israel was in possession of some 1,000 square-kilometres on top of the territory held on 11 June. The Arab pressure on Jerusalem had been greatly relieved and on 2 August the Israeli Government effectively annexed the city's Jewish part by appointing a 'military governor' to oversee its affairs. Though disappointed with the truce's timing, which prevented the IDF from consolidating its latest gains, Ben-Gurion began planning for the post-war situation: 'reducing the burden of the military budget ... Readiness for peace not necessarily on the basis of our existing force (which in my opinion allows the occupation of the whole of Palestine).'

Towards a military decision

Ben-Gurion's planning was premature. The fighting was far from over. In Jerusalem shelling, shooting and incursions into each other's territory were regular occurrences, as were Egyptian attacks on the Jewish convoys making their way to the Negev. In the central front the Iraqi contingent, now some 20,000 strong, continued to threaten the Israeli settlements in the Sharon and the coastal plain, while the ALA in the central Galilee was occasionally harassing local Israeli villages.

Things came to a head on 15 October 1948 when the IDF launched the largest offensive in the war until then and within a fortnight of heavy fighting re-established full communications with the Negev settlements. The offensive's immediate cause was the latest in a string of Egyptian attacks on Israeli supply convoys. Yet it reflected Ben-Gurion's growing fear that Israel's continued failure to assert its sovereignty over the area, ceded to it by the UN Partition Resolution, would result in its severance from the Jewish state. The British had long been trying to mobilise international support for the cession of the Negev to their Arab clients, Transjordan and Egypt, in contravention of the Partition Resolution. In

late September these efforts seemed to be crowned with success as the report of the UN Mediator to the Middle East, Count Folke Bernadotte of Sweden, published shortly after his assassination by Lehi extremists, recommended that the borders of the nascent Jewish and Arab states be revised to reflect the military situation on the ground: Israel would receive the entire Galilee, rather than part of it, while the Arabs would retain the far larger Negev.

This was totally unacceptable to Ben-Gurion, who viewed the Negev as Israel's strategic and demographic hinterland, a barren desert destined to be made to bloom, home to millions of prospective Jewish

On 22 December 1948, the IDF launched a large-scale offensive, code-named Operation Horev, and within a week expelled the Egyptian forces from Israeli territory and penetrated the Sinai Peninsula up to the strategic sire of Abu Ageila. (The State of Israel: The National Photo Collection)

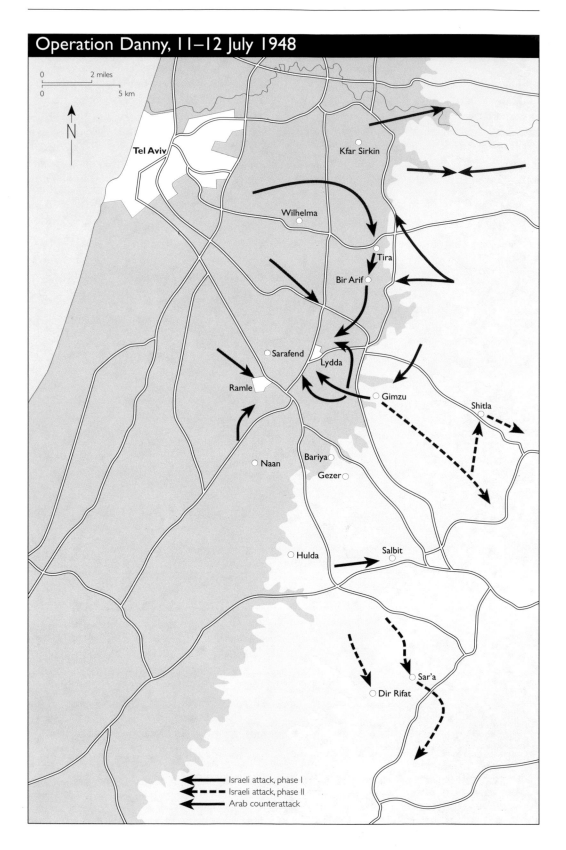

Operation Danny, 11–12 July 1948

0   2 miles
0   5 km

N

Tel Aviv

Kfar Sirkin

Wilhelma

Tira

Bir Arif

Sarafend

Lydda

Ramle

Gimzu

Shitla

Naan

Bariya

Gezer

Hulda

Salbit

Sar'a

Dir Rifat

Israeli attack, phase I
Israeli attack, phase II
Arab counterattack

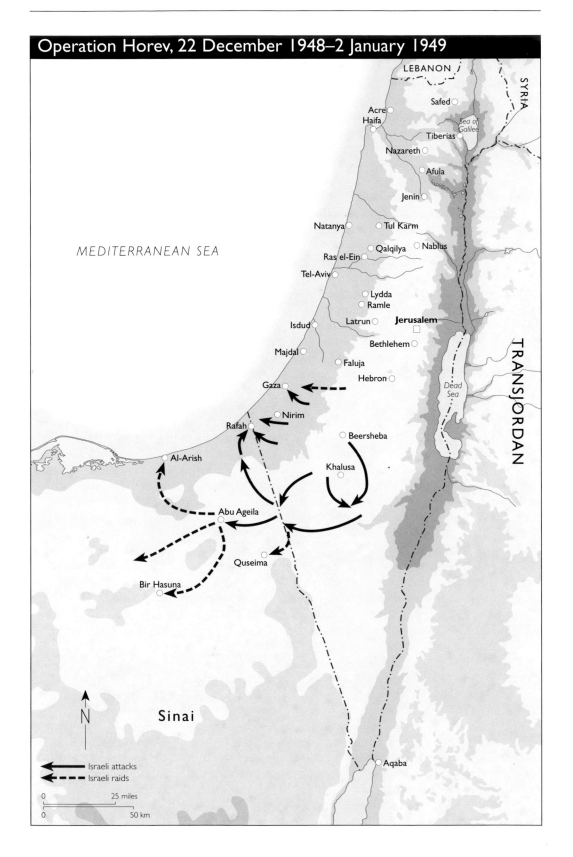

Operation Horev, 22 December 1948–2 January 1949

immigrants. He therefore approved the plan prepared by Yigael Yadin, the IDF's Acting chief of staff, and Yigal Allon, to break the Egyptian line of defence stretching from the Mediterranean to the Hebron Hills.

Code-named Operation Yoav (also known by its provisional name Operation Ten Plagues) and commanded by Allon, the offensive was carried out by a sizeable Israeli force of one armoured and three infantry brigades, with artillery and air support. Even the fledgling Israeli Navy participated in the operation by shelling Egyptian coastal installations, preventing naval resupply of enemy forces, and, most spectacularly, sinking the Egyptian flagship, the *Emir Farouq*.

Facing them was a 15,000-strong and well-fortified Egyptian force, consisting of two infantry brigades along the Rafah–Isdud axis; a reinforced brigade, holding the line eastward from Majdal to Beit Jibrin; and nine battalions of mostly Muslim Brothers irregulars holding the Auja–Beersheba–Hebron–Bethlehem axis. These were supported by two artillery regiments and an armoured battalion.

Yet for all its superiority in firepower and its strong entrenched position, the Egyptian deployment suffered from a major operational flaw – lack of depth in defence – which Allon exploited to the full. When the fighting was over by early November (a ceasefire was announced by the UN on 22 October but operations continued after that date), the Egyptians had been driven from their positions along the coastline, from Isdud to Gaza, and in the Judean and the Hebron Hills. Their extended line of defence was in tatters and the key town of Beersheba had fallen to the Israelis. An entire Egyptian brigade, some 4,000 troops with all its heavy equipment, was trapped in what would come to be known as the Faluja Pocket.

Emboldened by its success, the IDF proceeded to rout the Arab forces in the Galilee so as to secure Israel's position in the area. Mounted on the night of 28–29 October, Operation Hiram was carried out by a combined force of four infantry

brigades headed by Moshe Carmel, commander of the northern front. In 60 hours of fighting in which some 400 Arab fighters were killed and a similar number taken prisoner, the Israelis expelled the ALA and a Syrian battalion from the Upper Galilee, subsequently sweeping into Lebanon, capturing a number of border villages and reaching as far as the Litani River. As in the Negev, a hastily contrived UN ceasefire was arranged.

By now it had become increasingly clear to the Israelis that yet another major drive against Egypt would be required, as the latter refused to countenance peace negotiations, and continued to harass the Israeli settlements in the Negev as they sought to revamp their shattered presence in the area. When this was eventually mounted on 22 December, under the code-name of Operation Horev, it managed to clear the Egyptians from Israeli territory within five days, pursuing them into the Sinai Peninsula as far as Abu Ageila in the centre and al-Arish in the north. This incursion, however, brought Israel under intense international pressure, with Britain even threatening to invoke its 1936 bilateral treaty with Egypt. On 1 January 1949, Allon was ordered to evacuate Sinai within one day. Reluctant to let the opportunity to rout the Egyptian Army slip from his fingers, Allon managed to convince Ben-Gurion to approve an attack on the town of Rafah, south of Gaza, but not on al-Arish. This would be a far more demanding undertaking, given Rafah's superior defences, but would remove the danger of an Israeli–British confrontation while having the same strategic effect of bottling the Egyptian forces within the Gaza area. After a few days of fighting, the Israelis managed to capture the high ground around the town overlooking the road and the railway line to Sinai. By now the Egyptian Government had realised the threat to its forces and on 6 January announced its agreement to enter into armistice negotiations under UN mediation. The following day the guns on the southern front fell silent.

Trapped on the battlefield

There was no more serious defeat for the IDF during the Palestine War than the failure to capture the strategic police station in Latrun, at the foot of the Judean Hills overlooking the Tel-Aviv–Jerusalem road. On three occasions the IDF mounted large attacks on this heavily fortified and defended site, only to be beaten back with heavy casualties by the defending Arab Legion.

Participating in the first attack was a 20-year-old soldier by the name of Ariel Scheinerman, better known by his Hebrew name, Ariel (or Arik) Sharon. Born in 1928 in Kfar-Malal, a co-operative farming village 15 miles north-east of Tel-Aviv on the coastal Plain of Sharon, Arik was initiated into the Hagana at the tender age of 14. Three years later, in the summer of 1945, he undertook a squad leader course in a Negev kibbutz, before enrolling in the British-controlled Jewish Settlement Police. When hostilities broke out in late 1947, Arik was recruited again to the Hagana, as part of the Yishuv's general mobilisation drive. He participated in a number of raids on Arab targets, quickly rising in the ranks to become a platoon commander.

As the offensive against Latrun was being prepared, a battalion from the Alexandroni Brigade, to which Sharon's platoon belonged, was attached to the 7th Brigade which was to lead the assault. As they were travelling from their base in Netanya to Latrun, the soldiers watched with astonishment the usual bustle of civilian life in Tel-Aviv, before arriving at their concentration point near kibbutz Hulda. There they slept the night fitfully in an open field next to the road, listening to the drone of aeroplanes as they circled in the dark.

The next day they rested in an olive grove watching a group of young Jewish refugees, who had just arrived in the country from the British detention camps in Cyprus, undergoing a crash course in military training. As he was watching, Arik could not help wondering which of these young people, who had barely survived the Holocaust, would not be coming back. The next day the battalion's equipment arrived and the following night, 25 May, the battle was waged.

The Alexandroni battalion was assigned the primary task of pushing the Transjordanians off the height, then capturing a strategically located monastery and finally taking the police station and the village of Latrun. As Arik studied the map, he knew exactly how he would do it. Covered by the night, he would take his platoon up the left side of the hill, skirt the crown, then hit directly into the middle of the Transjordanian positions, taking them by surprise. With the battalion due to be in control of the heights by dawn, the capture of the monastery, directly beneath the newly captured Israeli positions, seemed a relatively easy task.

Tragically for the battalion, instead of attacking towards midnight under the cover of darkness, it reached its jumping-off position only at 4.00 am when the first rays of dawn had already appeared. 'While we waited, a nerve-racking half-hour turned into an hour, then one hour became two,' recalled Arik. 'As the night began to slip we sat on the buses and worried, beginning to dread what might happen if we were caught in front of the hill by the notoriously sudden Judean daylight.'

This fear turned out to be fully justified. As it disembarked from the buses and started its advance, five hours behind schedule, the battalion came under heavy machine-gun fire, with many of its soldiers wounded or killed. When the morning fog evaporated in

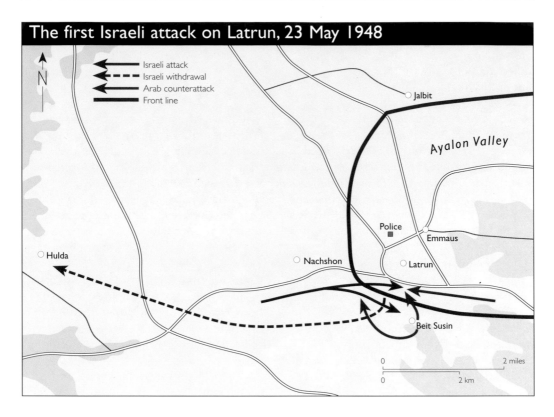

The first Israeli attack on Latrun, 23 May 1948

Israeli attack
Israeli withdrawal
Arab counterattack
Front line

N

Jalbit

Ayalon Valley

Police

Emmaus

Hulda   Nachshon   Latrun

Beit Susin

0   2 miles
0   2 km

a moment of startling swiftness, Arik's platoon found itself alone, caught in an open field, protected only by a shallow depression that gave it a degree of cover from the machine-gun and rifle fire pouring down from the Legion's positions on the hill. With its one radio smashed by an enemy bullet, the platoon was unable to communicate with the rest of the battalion, and had to hold out in anticipation of the resumption of the attack. In the worst-case scenario, Arik told his soldiers, they would have to wait until night when they would be able to escape.

The platoon had been in the gully for almost two hours when the Legion's fire increased in volume and tempo. On the hill in front of them the fighters saw Arab soldiers moving in their direction, firing as they ran, then disappearing into a neighbouring wadi. A few minutes later a line of them emerged from the wadi and from a vineyard in front of the platoon, crawling and firing. The fighters waited until the Arabs were within 30 or 40 yards,

then let loose a barrage of fire from their machine-guns, submachine guns and rifles. A moment later the Arabs were retreating into the wadi, carrying their wounded with them. Creeping on their stomachs, Arik and his soldiers pulled their wounded back to a small spring, where they braced themselves for the next assault.

This was not long in coming. In the next few hours the Arabs came again and again, each time the same way – moving in, shouting, firing. Around noon, the Arabs on the hill intensified their fire, the usual forerunner to another assault. Raising himself up to see what was happening, Arik felt something thud into his stomach, knocking him back. He heard himself say 'imah' – 'mother' – and immediately glanced around to see whether any of the men had heard him. Blood was seeping through his shirt and from his shorts, when he noticed another wound in his thigh. He lay down, still lucid, but feeling his strength ebbing away. Still, when two 'older' members of the platoon crawled to him, asking how he envisaged getting them away, he mustered enough strength to answer confidently: 'Look, I've gotten you out of a lot of tight places before. I'll get you out of this too.'

About one o'clock the Legion's fire seemed to have reduced in intensity. Arik knew something was happening but could not tell what it was, until it suddenly dawned on him that the platoon remained totally alone, the other units having withdrawn from the field. Arab villagers were moving over the hills behind, waving their weapons, and there was nothing that could save the platoon. By now, almost half of its fighters were dead and most of the others wounded, some critically. Arik saw the hopelessness in his men's eyes as he gave the order and pointed out the direction – straight back through the smoke and over the terraces. With any luck, the Legionnaires in front of them would keep their heads down; if they did not – they would all be dead before they reached the terraces.

The water in the spring where they were lying had long evaporated in the scorching sun, and the mud was already streaking red. Unable to contain his thirst, Arik crawled over to the spring and lowered his lips to the bloody puddle. He then crawled on all fours into the field, unable to get up. The rocks tore his knees as he made his way along the side of the first terrace behind the gully, but somehow he managed to keep crawling until

he reached the wall to the second. Blood was seeping from his trousers, and he knew there was no way he could clamber up on to the second terrace. On his hands and knees he struggled a few yards farther, then almost gave up when he saw a young boy from his platoon crawling up the slope on his left. Arik stared in horror at the boy, whose jaw had been shot up, leaving a mass of gore. At almost the same moment the boy saw Arik. Neither of them said a word. The boy was unable to talk, Arik was too weak. Then the boy began crawling next to Arik, keeping him moving, pushing him and supporting him over the terrace wall. Arik tried to tell him to go on and save himself, but he wouldn't leave.

Together the two crawled over one rocky terrace after another, their hands and knees burned from the charred earth. On the far side of the slopes they met more dazed stragglers. One of them, the deputy company commander, himself wounded, got his shoulder under Arik's arm, and leaning his weight on him kept him moving.

They walked like that for several miles through the smoke and fire. From time to time other figures stumbled out of the sooty haze, all of them moving in the direction of Hulda. Just before he lost consciousness Arik saw a jeep driving in and out of the blackened field searching for survivors. As it circled and drove close he recognised the girl driving and the boy sitting next to her as members of Kfar-Malal. A moment later he passed out.

The great game

'The invasion of Palestine by the Arab states was the first armed aggression which the world had seen since the end of the [Second World] War,' Trygve Lie, the first UN secretary-general wrote in his memoirs. 'The United Nations could not permit that aggression to succeed and at the same time survive as an influential force for peaceful settlement, collective security, and meaningful international law.'

A chain can only be as strong as its weakest link, and the UN as its least co-operative great power. As the only permanent members of the Security Council, the UN's executive arm, the Big Five – the United States, Britain, the Soviet Union, France and China – could and did exert disproportionate influence on the international politics of the nascent world organisation. The Soviet support for the idea of partition was instrumental in obtaining the necessary majority for the Partition Resolution, as were President Truman's exertions on its behalf. The relentless opposition to the idea by the British and the American foreign and defence establishments almost nipped it in the bud.

For policy-makers in London and Washington the idea of an independent Jewish state was anathema. As occupiers of vast territories endowed with natural resources (first and foremost oil) and sitting astride strategic waterways (for example, the Suez Canal) the Arabs had always been far more meaningful to Anglo-American interests than the Jews. Jewish national aspirations were merely a nuisance which unnecessarily marred relations with their Arab clients and had therefore to be neutralised. 'No solution of the Palestine problem should be proposed which would alienate the Arab states,' the British chiefs-of-staff advised the cabinet. For, if 'one of the

Vehemently opposed to the creation of a Jewish state, British Foreign Secretary Ernest Bevin did his utmost to prevent the adoption of the UN Partition Resolution and its implementation. (Topham Picturepoint)

two communities had to be antagonised, it was preferable, from the purely military angle, that a solution should be found which did not involve the continuing hostility of the Arabs; for in that event our difficulties would not be confined to Palestine but would extend throughout the whole of the Middle East.' And Sir John Troutbeck, Head of the British Middle East Office in Cairo, put it in even stronger terms:

We [and the Arabs] are partners in adversity on this question. A Jewish state is no more in our interest than it is in the Arabs ... Our whole strategy in the ME is founded upon holding a secure base in Egypt, but the usefulness of the base must be gravely impaired if we cannot move out of it except through hostile country.

To this must be added the deep concerns, especially by US Secretary of Defense James Forrestal, about the future availability of Middle-Eastern oil and the unquestioning belief that, if established, a Jewish state would become a Soviet outpost in the Middle East. Even President Truman, who overruled the view of his bureaucrats to support the establishment of a Jewish state and then to render it immediate *de facto* recognition, was sufficiently alarmed by this argument to dispatch a special envoy to Ben-Gurion to enquire whether Israel was going to become a 'red state'.

Obstructing the Partition Resolution

Although these fears proved to be largely misguided, they seemed real enough in the run-up to the General Assembly's vote and the subsequent months until the termination of the British Mandate to endanger the implementation of the Partition Resolution.

It was the British Government that proved the most formidable obstacle to partition. To be sure, the sudden American trusteeship proposal in March 1948 dealt

such a blow to UN prestige that Secretary-General Lie seriously considered resigning his post. But this episode pales in comparison with the sustained British effort to frustrate the will of the international community as expressed in the Partition Resolution. Though emerging from the Second World War a spent power, in its capacity as the occupying power of Palestine, Britain was uniquely poised to influence the country's future development.

Great Britain had placed the [Palestine] matter before the Assembly with the declared conviction that agreement between the Arabs and Jews was unattainable, wrote an evidently frustrated Trygve Lie. *This did not deter the British representative, [Colonial Secretary] Arthur Creech Jones, from informing the Assembly that Britain would give effect only to a plan accepted by the Arabs and the Jews ... The British approach proved to be not in accord, in my opinion, with either the letter or the spirit of the partition plan,* Lie added:

the United Kingdom could not progressively turn over authority to the Palestine Commission, as the Assembly resolution provided, but only abruptly and completely on 15 May. Neither did it 'regard favourably any proposal by the Commission to proceed to Palestine earlier than two weeks before the date of the termination of the Mandate'. London would not permit the formation of the militia which the Assembly's resolution called for, nor would it facilitate frontier delimitation. The Assembly had further recommended that the United Kingdom endeavour to evacuate by February 1 a seaport and hinterland in the area of the Jewish state adequate to provide facilities for immigration.

The British High Commissioner for Palestine, General Sir Alan Cunningham, was similarly exasperated with his government's obstructionism. 'It appears to me that H.M.G.'s policy is now simply to get out of Palestine as quickly as possible without regard to the consequences in Palestine,' he wrote to Creech Jones.

Cunningham's pleas fell on deaf ears. Having failed to prevent Palestine's smooth transition to statehood, the Foreign Office welcomed the pan-Arab invasion of the Jewish State as a golden opportunity to undo the UN Partition Resolution and cut Israel 'down to size'. Already in February 1948, following a meeting between the British

Foreign Secretary, Ernest Bevin, and
Transjordan's Prime Minister, Tawfiq Abu
al-Huda, in which the former acquiesced in a
Transjordanian invasion of Palestine after the

In late May 1948 the UN Mediator, Count Folke
Bernadotte (second left), arrived in the Middle East in
an attempt to bring about an end to the war. Israeli
militants assassinated him on 17 September. (Topham
Picturepoint)

termination of the Mandate, Bernard
Burrows, Head of the Foreign Office's Eastern
Department, commented that:

*It is tempting to think that Transjordan
might transgress the boundaries of the United
Nations' Jewish State to the extent of establishing
a corridor across the Southern Negev joining the
existing Transjordan territory to the Mediterranean
and Gaza. This would have immense strategic
advantages for us, both in cutting the Jewish State,
and therefore Communist influence, off from the
Red Sea and by extending up to the Mediterranean
the area in which our military and political
influence is predominant by providing a means of
sending necessary military equipment etc. into
Transjordan other than by the circuitous route
through Aqaba.*

On 20 May 1948, five days after the
Arab invasion, Bevin himself wrote to the
British Ambassador in Washington, Lord
Inverchapel:

*I do not (repeat not) intend in the near future
to recognise the Jewish State and still less to
support any proposal that it should become a
member of the United Nations. In this
connection I hope that even though the
Americans have recognised the Jewish State de
facto they will not commit themselves to any
precise recognition of boundaries. It might well
be that if the two sides ever accept a compromise
it would be on the basis of boundaries differing
from those recommended in the Partition Plan
of the General Assembly.*

That these border revisions were not
conceived in terms favourable to Israel, or for
that matter to the Palestinian Arabs (as early as
July 1946 Bevin had advised the Cabinet to
'assimilate' most of the Arab areas of Palestine
in Transjordan and Lebanon), was evidenced
by the tireless British attempts to convince the
UN Mediator, Count Folke Bernadotte, who
arrived in the Middle East at the end of May
1948, to devise a solution that would reduce
Israel to approximately the same size as that
envisaged by the 1937 Peel Partition Plan –
about half the size allotted to the Jewish state

by the UN Partition Resolution. The territories
assigned by the UN to the prospective Arab
state were to be incorporated into the
neighbouring Arab states.

Bernadotte was duly impressed. From the
beginning of his mission, he had been
echoing the British disparagement of the
Partition Resolution as a grave error that
had to be redressed in the near term.
When his plan was eventually published on
20 September 1948, shortly after his
assassination by Israeli militants, it bore the
traditional hallmarks of Foreign Office
thinking, namely: that an independent
Arab state in Palestine should not be
established and that most of its territory
should be annexed to Transjordan; that
Israel's territory should be greatly reduced;
that the port of Haifa should become an
international zone; and that Jewish
immigration to Israel should be regulated by
the UN. This last point, in particular, was
conspicuously modelled on the British
assessment, passed to Bernadotte, that the
Arab governments would never reconcile
themselves to the existence of an
independent Jewish state unless 'there
should be international agreement to accept
numbers of Jewish displaced persons
elsewhere than in Israel, and conceivably
also to limit immigration to Israel.'

Helping the Arabs

The British also sought to dictate the scope
and pace of the war operations by
controlling the levels of armament available
to both sides and by bringing about the
cessation of hostilities at critical junctures.

In December 1947, the US administration
suspended all arms shipments to the Middle
East in line with a UN arms embargo. This
move was favourably viewed by the British, as
it damaged Jewish efforts to arm themselves
while having practically no impact on the
Arab states, notably Transjordan, Egypt and
Iraq, which were armed and trained by
Britain. But by the beginning of 1948 Bevin
became increasingly concerned lest 'the

Jewish pressure for the lifting of the American embargo on the purchase of arms to the Jews in Palestine will become irresistible unless we are able to make an intelligent statement saying that we have decided upon a temporary suspension of deliveries of arms to the Arab states'. It went without saying that Britain was willing to continue arms deliveries to the Arab states, but it was doubtful whether:

this course would be the one most advantageous to the Arabs themselves ...The advantage which the Jews would obtain from a lifting of the American embargo in their favour would be out of all proportion to any advantage which the Arabs in Palestine could derive from our shipments to the Arab States. Whether or not the Palestine Government was able to prevent the delivery of arms to the Jews before May 15th we should have no right to interfere after that date.

This logic was sustained following the Arab invasion of Israel. At the initial stage of the war, when the Arabs went from strength to strength, the British collaborated with them in forestalling an immediate Security Council ceasefire resolution, both because it invoked the threat of sanctions against the Arab attackers under Chapter 7 (Article 39) of the UN Charter, and because the Arabs seemed well poised to make further territorial gains in Palestine.

Before long, however, the British changed their mind. The Arab states had secured substantial chunks of Palestine, reducing Israel's territory to a fraction of that awarded by the UN General Assembly: the entire Negev was in Arab hands, apart from a number of Jewish pockets; the Egyptian army was parked some 30 kilometres south of Tel-Aviv on the coastal plain and penetrated the Judean Desert up to the outskirts of Jerusalem; the Arab Legion occupied most of the Arab territory of Mandatory Palestine and was keeping the pressure on Jewish Jerusalem. Only in the Galilee did Israel occupy some territory awarded to the Arabs by the UN Resolution,

but even there the Arabs managed to hold on to a sizeable enclave in the central Galilee. Were the war to stop at this point, the British goal of 'Smaller Israel' would have fully materialised.

Another factor that drove Britain to change tack was the mounting public outrage in the United States over its attitude towards the war, and the distinct possibility that the arms embargo would be shortly lifted. On 20 May, the US Secretary of State, George Marshall, said in a press conference that 'the lifting of the embargo by the United States was under consideration'. Four days later Chaim Weizmann held a meeting with President Truman following which he stated that 'the President gave him hope that the United States would lift the embargo on the export of arms to the Middle East in the not too distant future'. On 26 May, congressman Jacob Javits introduced to the House of Representatives a measure, in the form of an amendment to the Greek–Turkish aid programme, to authorise a $100 million loan to Israel to provide military supplies and technical assistance. To make matters worse, the Senate Appropriations Committee demanded an official investigation to determine whether funds advanced to Britain were used to assist the Arab invasion of Israel, and whether US lend-lease equipment was being used for this purpose. The Chancellor of the Exchequer told the Cabinet:

that this enquiry might cause us some embarrassment, for, when we excluded Palestine and Transjordan from the sterling area, we had provided them with United States dollars with which to finance their current transactions. It seemed important that difficulties of this kind should not be allowed to affect the attitude of the United States Administration towards the flow of supplies to this country under the European Recovery Programme.

By this time the Foreign Office had become sufficiently alarmed to modify its truce resolution so as to bring about its immediate adoption by the Security Council. The original proposal, which called for a

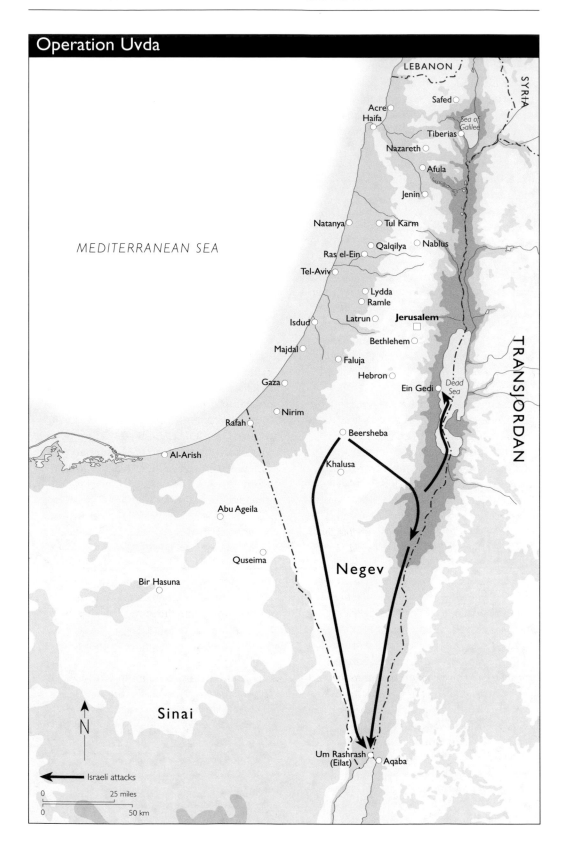

Operation Uvda

LEBANON

SYRIA

Acre
Haifa
Safed
Sea of Galilee
Tiberias
Nazareth
Afula
Jenin

MEDITERRANEAN SEA

Natanya
Tul Karm
Qalqilya
Nablus
Ras el-Ein
Tel-Aviv
Lydda
Ramle
Isdud
Latrun
Jerusalem
Bethlehem
Majdal
Faluja
Gaza
Hebron
Ein Gedi
Dead Sea
Nirim
Rafah
Beersheba
Al-Arish
Khalusa
Abu Ageila
Quseima
Bir Hasuna

Negev

Sinai

N

Um Rashrash (Eilat)
Aqaba

TRANSJORDAN

Israeli attacks

0   25 miles
0   50 km

four-week truce accompanied by a ban on the supply of arms to the belligerents and on the introduction of fighting men into the area, was doubtless designed to harm Israel rather than its Arab enemies. For one thing, due to the American embargo and the British naval blockade of Palestine up to the Arab attack, the Jews were overwhelmingly inferior to the invading Arab forces in terms of military equipment and war matériel; were the proposed arms embargo to be strictly applied, this qualitative imbalance would be perpetuated. For another thing, the ban on the introduction of fighting men into the area was exclusively designed to prevent a large influx of Jewish immigrants into Israel – a long-standing aim of British policy.

Though the British eventually acquiesced in the admission of Jewish refugees into Israel, provided that they did not undergo military training, they still believed that a truce would be in the Arab best interest, 'even from the point of view of influencing American opinion … I am convinced that the continuance of the truce will benefit the Arabs and that its breakdown would be disastrous from their point of view,' Bevin opined a few days before the truce was about to expire:

If they were responsible or could plausibly be represented as responsible for the renewal of fighting, it would probably be impossible for H.M. Govt. as a member of the United Nations to supply them with ammunition or indeed to give them any material assistance whatsoever. At the same time the Jews would be able to raise large sums of money in the United States and to purchase armaments either there or from other sources of supply. On the other hand the conditions now prevailing under the truce must be a source of grave embarrassment to the Jewish leaders. With much of their restricted manpower under arms and with serious interruption of their foreign trade their economic situation must be increasingly precarious.

Nor did the British Foreign Office content itself with the hope that the truce would mortally wound Israel by keeping Arab gains intact and ushering in a political settlement that would reduce the territory of the Jewish state well beyond that envisaged by the Partition Resolution. Instead it volunteered free advice to the Arab states on how to exploit this valuable respite to effect the diminution of the Israeli state. 'It might be presumed that the period of truce will be utilised by the Jews to establish an effective administration not only in those parts of their November State which are behind the military lines, but also in the Arab areas which they have occupied, such as the Central and Northern Galilee,' the Foreign Office cabled the British Ambassador to Egypt, Sir Ronald Campbell.

If the Arabs are to be in a position to bargain on equal terms, it is essential that they should also establish some real authority in the areas behind the lines occupied by their forces. This is particularly important in the area to the south of the Egyptian front line. The greater part of this area was awarded to the Jews last November and the Jewish settlements there are still holding out and presumably maintaining contact with Tel-Aviv. We shall have great difficulty in supporting the Arab claim to retain this part of Palestine unless it can be shown that it is in fact and not in name only under Arab administration during the truce …

When the Arabs failed to heed this advice and resumed hostilities the British did their utmost to stop the fighting, going so far as to send a military force to Aqaba and to state their readiness to fend off an Israeli incursion on Transjordanian territory. When Israel invaded the Sinai Peninsula, they threatened to invoke their 1936 bilateral treaty with Egypt unless the Israeli forces were not immediately withdrawn.

Leaving Jerusalem

Khalil Sakakini was one of the more colourful intellectuals of the Palestinian Arab community. Born in Jerusalem in 1878, he served for many years as a high official in the Palestine Education Department, leaving his mark on the country's Arabic education system. Like many of his co-religionists (he was an Orthodox Christian) who had lived for a millennium as a distinctly inferior minority under Islamic majority, in the wake of the collapse of the Ottoman Empire Sakakini embraced the ideal of 'Arab Nationalism', namely, that all Arabs are members of the same nation, regardless of their religion, as a means of social mobility and political integration. In 1920, he resigned his post at the Education Department because the British Government appointed a Jew, Sir Herbert Samuel, as its first High Commissioner for Palestine. Fifteen years later he built a house in the affluent Jerusalem neighbourhood of Qatamon and gave each room the name of an Arab capital: 'This is San'a, this is Damascus, this is Cordova, this is Baghdad, this is Cairo.'

As a leading educationalist, Sakakini introduced into the Arab curriculum a host of ardent nationalist themes, at times bordering on fascism. 'Power! Power! This is the new gospel that we must spread,' he wrote. 'He who is stronger in body, mind and spirit has a greater right to exist than he who is weak.' This principle, in Sakakini's opinion, condemned the Zionist enterprise to oblivion:

The Jews in their festivals lament and weep, since most of these festivals are in memorial of the disasters befalling them; while Muslim festivals are exhilarating events. A nation whose festivals are nothing but weeping has no future.

As fighting broke out in Palestine following the UN vote on partition and war reached Sakakini's doorstep, little was left of this confident bravado. 'We bade farewell to the previous year amidst the thunder of explosions,' he recorded in his diary on 1 January 1948, 'and this is how we have welcomed the new year: as if we are on the battlefield.' Two months later Sakakini seemed to be in the throes of despair. 'By God, I don't know how we will withstand the Jewish attacks,' he confided to his diary on 16 March. 'They are trained, organised, united and armed with the most modern weapons, while we have nothing of this. Has the time not come for us to understand that unity triumphs over factionalism, organisation over anarchy, and preparedness over neglect?'

This stark prognosis was further reinforced in mid-March following a meeting between a delegation from Qatamon and members of the AHC in the wake of Israeli retaliation against the neighbourhood:

We demanded weapons, recorded Sakakini, and they said that there weren't any. We asked for guards and they said: 'We don't have guards.' 'What shall we do then?' we asked. 'Buy arms and defend yourselves,' they answered. 'We don't have weapons, and should we buy ones, we don't have anyone who can use them,' we argued. After the blowing up of the Samiramis Hotel [on 5 January 1948], the Shahin House [9 March], and many other houses, who can guarantee that we won't be attacked yet again? It is your obligation – as the Arab Higher Committee – to provide us with arms and fighters. Where are the trained volunteers [from the Arab states]? Where is the money collected from all the Arab and Islamic countries?

Several days later, the Qatamon delegation was visited by Abd al-Qader al-Husseini and his chief lieutenants and Sakakini took the opportunity to lecture them on the universal laws of war that had to be strictly observed: the wounded must be well tended; soldiers must be treated properly; the bodies of the dead must be returned to their families. In short, he argued, 'we must abide by the order of Abu Bakr [the first Caliph after Prophet Muhammad] when he bade farewell to the army on its way to Palestine:

"Thou shall not kill a child, an old man, or a woman; thou shalt not burn a tree or destroy a house; thou shalt not pursue he who flees and thou shalt not mutilate bodies, nor harm the one who is involved in the worship of God."

As Husseini remained unimpressed by what apparently seemed to him as romantic notions of chivalry, the exasperated Sakakini wrote in his diary:

Had I been able to speak my mind, I would have told them: 'Return your swords to their scabbards and don't fight anyone; there is enough room in the world for everyone.' But who would listen to these words or pay them any attention. So let me just reiterate Jesus's words: 'My kingdom is not of this world.'

Husseini's visit brought no respite to Qatamon. Shortly after his departure, during the evening of Saturday 20 March, an increasingly desperate Sakakini recorded in his diary:

The whistle of the bullets and the thunder of the shells do not stop day or night. We heard nothing like that during the two world wars. Every time we enter our homes we expect them to be shelled and fall on our heads; every time we walk the streets we keep close to the walls and the sandbags for fear of a stray bullet ... In this situation it is hardly surprising that the residents

are considering moving to another neighbourhood or another city in order to free themselves of this permanent anxiety and danger ... This is why many of our neighbours had moved either to the Old City, or to Beit Jalla, or to Amman, Cairo, or other places. Only a handful of affluent people remained: our family, the Saruji brothers, Daoud Talil, and Yusuf Abdu.

On 7 April, having found a bullet on his balcony, Sakakini tried to brave the situation. 'I assumed that we were safe since our house is at the heart of the quarter, with neighbouring houses surrounding it like a wall,' he wrote, 'only to find ourselves exposed to bullets. From now on we will exercise greater care: The believer is not hit twice by the same stone.'

There was, however, little comfort in store. On 9 April, Sakakini sadly recorded the death of al-Husseini in the battle for the Kastel:

Today Abd al-Qader, God's blessings be upon him, was buried. Palestine has never seen such a huge funeral. If there is one person who deserves the epithet: 'The entire country went behind his cascade,' it is Abd al-Qader: you could walk the streets and see not a single shop open. Never have all the shops closed down and the markets emptied as was the case today.

On 13 April Sakakini felt that enough was enough:

The artillery shelling and machine-gun fire do not stop day or night, as if we were on an ever heating battlefield ... Night falls and we cannot close our eyes. We say that if we live to see the day, we will leave this neighbourhood, Qatamon, to another, or leave this country altogether.

A fortnight later Sakakini left Jerusalem for Cairo with his two daughters. He died there on 13 August 1953.

From ceasefire to armistice

On 13 January 1949, six days after the fighting between their armies had ended, Egyptian and Israeli representatives met for armistice negotiations on the Mediterranean island of Rhodes, where the UN Mediator, Count Folke Bernadotte, had set up his headquarters in the previous summer. Six weeks later, on 24 February, the two countries signed an agreement which formally ended hostilities between them and established an armistice line along the international border. Skilfully mediated by Ralph Bunche, who succeeded Bernadotte as Acting Mediator following the latter's assassination, the agreement constituted a balanced compromise between the maximum positions of both sides. Egypt freed its besieged brigade in Faluja, gained control over what would hitherto be known as the Gaza Strip, and forced Israel to accept a demilitarised zone in the Auja area, on the international border. For its part Israel consolidated its control over the northern Negev, including Beersheba, and was effectively given a free hand to assert its sovereignty over the rest of the Negev, in line with the UN Partition Resolution, without violating its agreement with Egypt.

The importance of the Egyptian–Israeli agreement cannot be overstated. Three months earlier, on 16 November, the Security Council had passed a resolution urging the belligerents to negotiate armistice agreements, either directly or through UN mediation. But the resolution had remained a dead letter as Israel and Egypt had not yet settled their scores, while the rest of the Arab states would not make the first move. Now that the largest Arab country had made its truce with the Jewish state, the rest of the Arabs quickly followed suit.

Negotiations between Israel and Lebanon began on 3 March at the scenic site of Rosh Haniqra, on the Israeli–Lebanese border, and were successfully completed within three weeks. Conspicuously lacking the distrust and acrimony that had characterised much of the Egyptian–Israeli talks, the Israeli–Lebanese

dialogue hardly involved any contentious issues. Both parties agreed that the armistice line should run along the international border and that upon conclusion of the agreement Israel would withdraw from whatever Lebanese territories it had occupied. That despite this fundamental unanimity three weeks were required for the agreement to be finalised was due to Israel's insistence to link its withdrawal from Lebanon with Syria's evacuation of all Israeli territories occupied during the war.

This, however, was easier said than done. Starting on 5 April and lasting three full months, the Syrian–Israeli negotiations proved the most protracted and arduous of all armistice talks between Israel and its Arab adversaries. The situation was further

On 13 January 1949, Egyptian and Israeli representatives met for negotiations on the Mediterranean island of Rhodes. Six weeks later they signed an agreement which ended hostilities between their countries and established an armistice line along the international border. (The State of Israel: The National Photo Collection)

complicated by a military coup in Damascus on 30 March, shortly after the government had announced its readiness to negotiate with Israel. Anxious to shore up his fledgling regime, the newly installed ruler, Colonel Husni Zaim, subordinated the armistice negotiations (and for that matter any other aspect of his policy at home and abroad) to the overriding consideration of his own political survival. This manifested itself, on the one hand, in the categorical rejection of Israel's demand for Syrian withdrawal to the international border, and, on the other, in occasional allusions to the possibility of direct peace talks with the Israeli Prime Minister, David Ben-Gurion.

Though viewing these allusions as a bargaining chip aimed at buying Syria international sympathy and improving its position in the armistice negotiations, Ben-Gurion was sufficiently intrigued to suggest that senior Israeli decision-makers, including Foreign Minister Moshe Sharett, meet with the Syrian leader. Meanwhile he instructed the Israeli delegation to the armistice talks 'to inform the Syrians in clear terms that first of all – an armistice agreement on the basis of the previous international line. And then – discussion of peace and alliance. We will be prepared for maximum cooperation.'

As the Syrians seemed to be taking heed of the Israeli position, Ben-Gurion became cautiously optimistic:

In a conversation with a Swiss writer Zaim stated that he wanted peace with Israel, he recorded in his diary on 9 July. *In my opinion we should cling to this statement. The fact that Zaim is prepared for an armistice based on complete withdrawal to the international border proves that for one reason or another he wants good relations with us ... If the armistice agreement with Syria will be signed this week ... it is desirable that [Elias] Sasson [a leading Israeli negotiator with Arab leaders] will go to Damascus to check the ground.*

In the event, the armistice agreement of 20 July 1949 turned out to be the farthest limit of the Syrian–Israeli reconciliation.

Three weeks later Zaim was overthrown by yet another military coup and summarily executed, with his initiative dying with him. Indeed, already before his demise, perhaps for fear of a domestic backlash, Zaim began backtracking from his initiative. Shortly after the signing of the armistice agreement, he passed a message to the Israelis, through the good offices of the UN mediation team, that 'he would like the matter to be postponed for several weeks, [as] he did not wish to breach the wall of Arab unity'.

It was thus left to King Abdallah of Transjordan to demonstrate the most receptiveness to the idea of a lasting accommodation with the Jewish state. As early as October 1948 he had indicated his readiness for a deal with Israel, only to be obstructed by the British, who would not have any agreement that did not involve substantial Israeli concessions. 'I admit the overwhelming necessity for Transjordan to make peace with the Jews,' the British Acting Consul-General in Jerusalem, Sir Hugh Dow, commented in December 1948:

If however, there is uncertainty on this question of the Negev, it appears to me to be undesirable from our point of view to allow King Abdallah to push his negotiations with the Jews to anything like a conclusive stage ... the Negev is of little value to the Arabs while of strategic value to us, and King Abdallah may well be content to let the Jews have it the moment he sees that he has no prospect of getting Gaza.

Sir Hugh's fears were premature. Israel at the time was not yet prepared to acquiesce in Abdallah's long-standing ambition to annex whatever he could of the territory assigned to the Arab state by the Partition Resolution. This view was relayed to the king by Golda Meir during their meeting in November 1947 and it remained the official Israeli position during the Palestine War. 'Our main objective now is peace ... which is why I support talking to Abdallah,' Prime Minister Ben-Gurion told his advisers on 18 December 1948, 'but we should clarify [to him] from the start that ... we will not be able to agree

Israeli and Transjordanian Jerusalem commanders, Lieutenant Colonel Moshe Dayan and Major Abdallah al-Tel, oversee an exchange of prisoners-of-war, February 1949. (The State of Israel: The National Photo Collection)

lightly to the annexation of [the Arab] parts of Palestine to Transjordan.'

Though the Israelis would eventually relent in their opposition to Abdallah's occupation of the territory that would come to be known as the West Bank (of the Hashemite Kingdom), they would not do so before reducing its scope in their favour. Through a successful combination of political and military means, including the implicit threat to resume hostilities, Israel extended the armistice line eastward at the centre of the country by gaining control over both the Iraqi-held Sharon territory and the Wadi Ara area, thus bringing the entire Afula–Hadera road under its control. It also asserted its sovereignty over the southern Negev, by sending a military force to capture Eilat, on the northern tip of the Gulf of Aqaba, and managed to have the international border in the Araba established as the armistice line. Only in Latrun and Jerusalem did Israel fail to achieve its objectives of dislodging the Arab Legion and gaining free access to such sites as the Wailing Wall, the ancient Jewish cemetery on Mount Olive and the Hebrew University and Hadassah Hospital on Mount Scopus. Still, there is little doubt as to who was the victor of the Palestine War. Having violently rejected the Partition Resolution of November 1947, the Arabs were now effectively forced to acquiesce in the reality of a Jewish state stretching over larger

The 1949 Armistice lines

LEBANON
SYRIA
Haifa
Sea of Galilee
MEDITERRANEAN
SEA
Jordan
Tel Aviv
Jaffa
THE WEST BANK
TRANS-JORDAN
Jerusalem
Gaza
Dead Sea
ISRAEL
EGYPT
Negev
N
Sinai
Aqaba
0   25 miles
0   50 km
– · – · – Armistice line 1949

territories than that assigned to it by the General Assembly. For decades to come they would attempt to undo these setbacks.

Perpetuating the Arab-Israeli conflict

'The Palestinians had neighbouring Arab states which opened their borders and doors to the refugees, while the Jews had no alternative but to triumph or to die,' Muhammad Nimr al-Khatib, a prominent Palestinian leader during the 1948 War, summed up his nation's defeat and dispersion. Writing from the Israeli perspective, journalists Jon and David Kimche similarly pinned the source of Israel's victory on 'the will to survive on the part of the Palestinian Jews, and perhaps even more, the political and military expression of this will in the person of Israel's first Prime Minister, David Ben-Gurion, and the military instruments of Palestinian Jewry: the Hagana, its clandestine national defence organisation, and the Palmach, the hand-picked striking force which together provided the foundation and framework of the future Israeli Defence Forces.'

This prognosis is well taken. If anything, the Palestine War demonstrates that there is far more to armed conflict than the size of the armies engaged in combat operations or the nature of their equipment. That war was not won by the militarily stronger combatant: had this been the case, the far better armed and organised Arab armies would have readily defeated the poorly equipped and widely dispersed Israeli forces before they had the chance to equip themselves during the first truce. Rather it was a clash of national wills in which the more resilient society prevailed. In 1948, both the Jewish and the Arab communities in Palestine were thrown into a whirlpool of hardship, dislocation and all-out war – conditions that no society can survive without the absolute commitment of its most vital élites. Yet while the atomised Palestinian Arab community, lacking a cohesive corporate identity, fragmented into

small pieces, the Yishuv managed to weather the storm by extreme effort: its 6,000 fatalities, a full one per cent of the total Jewish population, were heavier in relative (if not absolute) terms than those of any of its Arab adversaries, including the Palestinians.

Neither did the Arab states throw their full weight and whole-hearted commitment behind the Palestine War. As the report of an Iraqi parliamentary committee of inquiry into the war put it in September 1949:

It is a general rule that national independence cannot be obtained by reliance on great-power sympathy or pity. World sympathy is exclusively determined by power criteria and cost-benefit considerations, and the international community will acquiesce only in a fait accompli. Seven Arab states – in control of vast strategic territories and abundant oil and other natural resources, and enjoying the sympathy of an omnipotent Muslim World – lost Palestine merely because of their reliance on romantic notions of legality and justice. Culpability for the loss of Palestine does indeed lie with some of the Arab leaders who lacked the will and the capacity for self-sacrifice.

The birth of the Palestinian refugee problem

Even before the outbreak of hostilities, many Palestinian Arabs had already fled their homes. Still larger numbers left before war reached their doorstep. By April 1948, a month before Israel's declaration of independence, and at a time when the Arabs appeared to be winning the war, some 100,000 Palestinians, mostly from the main urban centres of Jaffa, Haifa and Jerusalem and from villages in the coastal plain, had gone. Within another month those numbers had nearly doubled; and by early

June, according to an internal Hagana report, some 390,000 Palestinians had left. By the time the fighting was over in early 1949, the number of refugees had risen to between 550,000 and 600,000.

Why did such vast numbers of Palestinians take to the road? There were the obvious reasons commonly associated with war: fear, disorientation, economic privation. But to these must be added the local Palestinians' disillusionment with their own leadership, the role taken by that leadership in forcing widespread evacuations and, perhaps above all, a lack of communal cohesion or of a willingness, especially at the highest levels, to subordinate personal interest to the general good.

On this last point, a number of Palestinians have themselves spoken eloquently. 'There was a Belgian ship,' recalls the academic Ibrahim Abu Lughod, who fled Jaffa in 1948:

and one of the sailors, a young man, looked at us – and the ship was full of people from

Jaffa, some of us were young adults – and he said, 'Why don't you stay and fight?' I have never forgotten his face and I have never had one good answer for him.

Another former resident of Jaffa was the renowned Palestinian intellectual Hisham Sharabi, who in December 1947 left for the United States. Three decades later he asked himself: 'How could we leave our country when a war was raging and the Jews were gearing themselves to devour Palestine?' His answer:

There were others to fight on my behalf; those who had fought in the 1936 revolt and who would do the fighting in the future. They were peasants ... [whose] natural place was here, on

The foremost tragedy of the Palestine War was the collapse and dispersion of Palestinian Arab society, with nearly half of its members becoming refugees elsewhere in Palestine or in neighbouring Arab states. (The State of Israel: The National Photo Collection)

this land. As for us – the educated ones – we were on a different plane. We were struggling on the intellectual front.

In fact, the Palestinian peasants proved no more attached to the land than the educated classes. Rather than stay behind and fight, they followed in the footsteps of their urban brothers and took to the road from the first moments of the hostilities. Still, the lion's share of culpability for the Palestinian collapse and dispersion undoubtedly lies with the 'educated ones', whose lack of national sentiment, so starkly portrayed by Sharabi and Abu Lughod, set in train the entire Palestinian exodus. The moment its leading members chose to place their own safety ahead of all other considerations, the exodus became a foregone conclusion.

The British High Commissioner for Palestine, General Sir Alan Cunningham, summarised what was happening with quintessential British understatement:

The collapsing Arab morale in Palestine is in some measure due to the increasing tendency of those who should be leading them to leave the country ... For instance in Jaffa the Mayor went on four days' leave 12 days ago and has not returned, and half the National Committee has left. In Haifa the Arab members of the municipality left some time ago; the two leaders of the Arab Liberation Army left actually during the recent battle. Now the Chief Arab Magistrate has left. In all parts of the country the effendi class has been evacuating in large numbers over a considerable period and the tempo is increasing.

Hussein Khalidi, Secretary of the Arab Higher Committee, was more forthright. 'In 1936 there were 60,000 [British] troops and [the Arabs] did not fear,' he complained to the Mufti on 2 January 1948. 'Now we deal with 30,000 Jews and [the Arabs] are trembling in fear.' Ten days later, he was even more scathing. 'Forty days after the declaration of a jihad, and I am shattered,' he complained to a fellow Palestinian. 'Everyone has left me. Six [AHC members] are in Cairo, two are in Damascus – I won't

be able to hold on much longer ... Everyone is leaving. Everyone who has a check or some money – off he goes to Egypt, to Lebanon, to Damascus.'

The desertion of the élites had a domino effect on the middle classes and the peasantry. But huge numbers of Palestinians were also driven out of their homes by their own leaders and/or by Arab military forces, whether out of military considerations or, more actively, to prevent them from becoming citizens of the nascent Jewish State. In the largest and best-known example of such a forced exodus, tens of thousands of Arabs were ordered or bullied into leaving the city of Haifa against their wishes on the instructions of the AHC, despite sustained Jewish efforts to convince them to stay. Only days earlier, thousands of Arabs in Tiberias had been similarly forced out by their own leaders. In Jaffa, the largest Arab community of Mandatory Palestine, the municipality organised the transfer of thousands of residents by land and sea, while in the town of Beisan in the Jordan valley, the women and children were ordered out as the Arab Legion dug in. And then there were the tens of thousands of rural villagers who were likewise forced out of their homes by order of the AHC, local Arab militias or the armies of the Arab states.

None of this is to deny that Israeli forces did on occasion expel Palestinians. But this accounted for only a small fraction of the total exodus, occurred not within the framework of a premeditated plan but in the heat of battle, and was dictated predominantly by ad hoc military considerations (notably the need to deny strategic sites to the enemy if there were no available Jewish forces to hold them). It will be recalled that the Hagana's military plan for rebuffing an anticipated pan-Arab invasion (Plan D) was predicated, in the explicit instructions of Israel Galili, the Hagana's chief-of-staff on the 'acknowledgement of the full rights, needs, and freedom of the Arabs in the Hebrew state without any discrimination, and a desire for co-existence on the basis of mutual freedom and dignity'. Indeed, even the largest of the Israeli expulsions, during the battle for Lydda in July 1948, emanated from a string of unexpected developments on the ground and was in no way foreseen in military plans for the capture of the town or reflected in the initial phase of its occupation. It was only when the occupying forces encountered stiffer resistance than expected that they decided to 'encourage' the population's departure to Arab-controlled areas, a few miles to the east, so as not to leave a hostile armed base at the rear of the Israeli advance and to clog the main roads in order to forestall a possible counter-attack by the Arab Legion.

It is true that neither the AHC nor the Arab states envisaged a Palestinian dispersion of the extent that occurred, and that both sought to contain it once it began snowballing. But it is no less true that they acted in a way that condemned hundreds of thousands of Palestinians to exile. As early as September 1947, more than two months before the passing of the UN Partition Resolution, an Arab League summit in the Lebanese town of Sofar urged the Arab states to 'open their doors to Palestinian children, women, and the elderly and to fend for them, should the developments in Palestine so require'.

This recommendation was endorsed the following month by a gathering of Haifa's Arab leadership and reiterated by the Mufti in person in January 1948. For his part King Abdallah reportedly promised that 'if any Palestine Arabs should become refugees as a result of the Husseini faction's activities, the gates of Transjordan would always be open to them'.

The logic behind this policy was apparently that 'the absence of the women and children from Palestine would free the men for fighting', as the Secretary-General of the Arab League, Abd al-Rahman Azzam put it. This thinking, nevertheless, proved to be disastrously misconceived. Far from boosting morale and freeing the men for fighting, the mass departure of women and children led to the total depopulation of towns and villages as the men preferred to join their families rather than stay behind and fight.

In recognition of its mistake, in early March 1948, the AHC issued a circular castigating the flight out of the country as a blemish on both 'the jihad movement and the reputation of the Palestinians', and stating that 'in places of great danger, women, children, and the elderly should be moved to safer areas' within Palestine. But only a week later, the AHC itself was evidently allowing those same categories of persons to leave Jerusalem for Lebanon and also ordering the removal of women and children from Haifa. By late April, nothing remained of the AHC's stillborn instruction as Transjordan threw its doors open to the mass arrival of Palestinian women and children and the Arab Legion was given a free hand to carry out population transfers at its discretion.

An Arab betrayal?

Success has many parents while failure is an orphan. The magnitude of the Arab defeat and the scale of the Palestinian dispersion triggered immediate and bitter recriminations between the Palestinians and their supposed saviours. From the moment of their arrival in the 'neighbouring Arab states which opened their borders and doors', tension between the refugees and the host societies ran high. The former considered the states derelict for having issued wild promises of military support on which they never made good. The latter regarded the Palestinians as a cowardly lot who had shamefully deserted their homeland while expecting others to fight for them.

This mutual animosity was also manifest within Palestine itself, where the pan-Arab volunteer force that entered the country in early 1948 found itself at loggerheads with the community it was supposed to defend. Denunciations and violent clashes were common, with the local population often refusing to provide the ALA with the basic necessities for daily upkeep and military operations, and army personnel abusing their Palestinian hosts, of whom they were openly contemptuous. When an Iraqi officer in Jerusalem was asked to explain his persistent refusal to greet the local populace, he angrily retorted that 'one doesn't greet these dodging dogs, whose cowardice causes poor Iraqis to die'.

In a report on the situation in Palestine written in late March 1948, Ismail Safwat charged the Palestinian Arabs of remaining embroiled in their internal squabbles as if there was no existential threat to their corporate identity. Special bitterness was reserved for the Mufti and his local supporters, whose self-serving behaviour was largely culpable for the polarisation and fragmentation of Palestinian society. 'Recent reports prove that the Palestinians are arming themselves not for the war against the Jews but rather to subdue their Arab adversaries or to protect themselves from perceived Arab enemies,' Safwat wrote. 'I have done everything within my power to overcome this regrettable state of affairs, to no avail. The situation is deteriorating by the day and its persistence is certain to entail dire consequences.'

Similar indictments of the Palestinians were voiced throughout the Arab world. 'Fright has struck the Palestinian Arabs and they fled their country,' commented Radio Baghdad on the eve of the pan-Arab invasion of Israel. 'These are hard words indeed, yet they are true.' And the Lebanese Minister of the Interior, Camille Chamoun, did not mince his words either. 'The people of Palestine, in their previous resistance to imperialists and Zionists, proved they were worthy of independence,' he argued. 'But at this decisive stage of the fighting they have not remained so dignified in their stand; they lack organisation and omitted to arm themselves as well as their enemy did. Many of them did not assist their brothers from nearby Arab countries who hastened to help them.'

In Syria, Lebanon and Transjordan there were repeated calls during the war for the return of the refugees to Palestine or, at the very least, of young men of military age, many of whom had arrived under the pretext of volunteering for the ALA. When occasional restrictions in Syria and Lebanon on the entry of males between the ages of 16 and 50 drove many Palestinians to Egypt, they were often received with disdain. 'Why should we go to Palestine to fight while Palestine Arab fighters are deserting the cause by flight to Egypt,' was the local reaction in Alexandria upon the arrival of several refugee ships from Haifa in late April 1948.

The Palestinians did not hesitate to reply in kind. In a letter to the Syrian representative at the UN, Jamal al-Husseini argued that 'the regular [Arab] armies did not enable the inhabitants of the country to defend themselves, but merely facilitated their escape from Palestine'. The prominent Palestinian leader Emile Ghoury was even more outspoken. In an interview with the London *Telegraph* in August 1948 he blamed the Arab states for the creation of the refugee problem; as did the organisers of protest demonstrations that took place in many West Bank towns on the first anniversary of Israel's establishment. During a fact-finding mission to Gaza in June 1949, Sir John Troutbeck, head of the British Middle-East office in Cairo and no friend to Israel or the Jews, was surprised to discover that, while the refugees:

express no bitterness against the Jews (or for that matter against the Americans or ourselves) they speak with the utmost bitterness of the Egyptians and other Arab states. 'We know who our enemies are,' they will say, and they are referring to their Arab brothers who, they declare, persuaded them unnecessarily to leave their homes ... I even heard it said that many of the refugees would give a welcome to the Israelis if they were to come in and take the district over.

The prevailing conviction among the refugees that they had been the victims of their fellow Arabs rather than of Israeli aggression was grounded not only in their personal experience but in the larger facts of inter-Arab politics. Indeed, had the Jewish State lost the war, its territory would not have been handed over to the Palestinians but rather divided among the invading forces, for the simple reason that none of the Arab régimes viewed the Palestinians as a distinct nation. As the American academic Philip Hitti put the Arab view to a joint Anglo-American commission of inquiry in 1946: 'There is no such thing as Palestine in history, absolutely not.'

This fact was keenly recognised by the British authorities as they were departing from Palestine. In mid-December 1947, for example, they estimated that 'as events are at the moment it does not appear that Arab Palestine will be an entity, but rather that the Arab countries will each claim a portion in return for their assistance, unless King Abdallah takes rapid and firm action as soon as the British withdrawal is completed.' A couple of months later, High

Commissioner Cunningham informed Colonial Secretary Creech Jones that 'the most likely arrangement seems to be Eastern Galilee to Syria, Samaria and Hebron to Abdallah, and the South to Egypt, and it might well end in annexation of this pattern, the centre remains uncertain'.

Perhaps the best proof of British prescience regarding this matter was that neither Egypt nor Jordan ever allowed Palestinian self-determination in the parts of Palestine they conquered during the 1948 War: respectively, Gaza and the West Bank. As the Egyptian representative to the armistice talks told a British journalist: 'We don't care if all the refugees will die. There are enough Arabs around.' More than half a century later, many of these refugees still languish in squalid camps waiting for their problem to be solved.

Further reading

Alami, Musa, 'The Lessons of Palestine', *Middle East Journal*, October 1949.

Collins, Larry, and Lapierre, Dominique, *O Jerusalem*, New York, 1972.

Herzog, Chaim, *The Arab-Israeli Wars: War and Peace in the Middle East*, New York, 1982.

Karsh, Efraim, *Fabricating Israeli History: The 'New Historians'*, London, 2000.

Khalaf, Issa, *Politics in Palestine: Arab Factionalism and Social Disintegration 1939–1948*, Albany, 1991.

Khalidi, Rashid, *Palestinian Identity: The Construction of Modern National Consciousness*, New York, 1997.

Khalidi, Walid, ed., *From Haven to Conquest*, Beirut, 1971.

— *Palestine Reborn*, London, 1992.

Kimche, Jon and David, *Both Sides of the Hill: The Arab–Jewish War and the Founding of the State of Israel*, London, 1969.

Kurzman, Dan, *Genesis 1948: the First Arab–Israeli War*, New York, 1970.

Laqueur, Walter, *A History of Zionism*, New York, 1972.

Lorch, Netanel, *The Edge of the Sword: Israel's War of Independence 1947–1949*, Jerusalem, 1968.

Index

Figures in **bold** refer to illustrations

Related titles from Osprey Publishing

ELITE (ELI)
Uniforms, equipment, tactics and personalities of troops and commanders

MEN-AT-ARMS (MAA)
Uniforms, equipment, history and organisation of troops

CAMPAIGN (CAM)
Strategies, tactics and battle experiences of opposing armies

ESSENTIAL HISTORIES (ESS)
Concise overviews of major wars and theatres of war

NEW VANGUARD (NVG)
Design, development and operation of the machinery of war

WARRIOR (WAR)
Motivation, training, combat experiences and equipment of individual soldiers

ORDER OF BATTLE (OOB)
Unit-by-unit troop movements and command strategies of major battles
Contact us for more details – see below

AIRCRAFT OF THE ACES (ACES)
Experiences and achievements of 'ace' fighter pilots

AVIATION ELITE (AEU)
Combat histories of fighter or bomber units
Contact us for more details – see below

COMBAT AIRCRAFT (COM)
History, technology and crews of military aircraft
Contact us for more details – see below

To order any of these titles, or for more information on Osprey Publishing, contact:
Osprey Direct (UK) *Tel:* +44 (0)1933 443863 *Fax:* +44 (0)1933 443849 *E-mail:* info@ospreydirect.co.uk
Osprey Direct (USA) c/o MBI Publishing *Toll-free:* 1 800 826 6600 *Phone:* 1 715 294 3345
Fax: 1 715 294 4448 *E-mail:* info@ospreydirectusa.com
www.ospreypublishing.com